THE POCKET TREASURY
OF INSPIRATIONAL VERSE

THE POCKET TREASURY
OF
INSPIRATIONAL
VERSE

FRONTPORCH

BOOKS

The Pocket Treasury of Inspirational Verse
Copyright 1999 by FrontPorch Books, a division of Garborgs.
Published by Garborgs
P.O. Box 20132, Bloomington, MN 55420
To order call 800/678-5727

Scripture quotations are taken from the Holy Bible, King James Version

Produced for Garborgs by The Livingstone Corporation.
Project Staff include: Paige Haley, Nicole Poppe, Shari TeSlaa,
Christopher D. Hudson.

Printed and bound in the United States of America.

Table of Contents

THE BONDS OF LOVE 43

THE PASSAGE OF TIME 167

Love and Eternity

To My Dear and Loving Husband

ANNE BRADSTREET

If ever two were one, then surely we.
If ever man were loved by wife, then thee;
If ever wife was happy in a man,
Compare with me, ye women, if you can.
I prize thy love more than whole mines of gold
Or all the riches that the East doth hold.
My love is such that rivers cannot quench,
Nor ought but love from thee, give recompense.
Thy love is such I can no way repay,
The heavens reward thee manifold, I pray.
Then while we live, in love let's so persevere
That when we live no more, we may live ever.

When, Dearest, I but Think of Thee

SIR JOHN SUCKLING

When, dearest, I but think of thee,
Me thinks all things that lovely be
Are present, and my soul delighted:
For beauties that from worth arise
Are like the grace of deities,
Still present with us, tho' unsighted.
Thus while I sit and sigh the day
With all his borrow'd lights away,
Till night's black wings do overtake me,
Thinking on thee, thy beauties then,
As sudden lights do sleepy men,
So they by their bright rays awake me.
Thus absence dies, and dying proves
No absence can subsist with loves
That do partake of fair perfection:
Since in the darkest night they may
By love's quick motion find a way
To see each other by reflection.
The waving sea can with each flood
Bathe some high promont that hath stood
Far from the main up in the river:
O think not then but love can do
As much! for that's an ocean too,
Which flows not every day, but ever!

3

Sonnets from the Portuguese
XIV

ELIZABETH BARRETT BROWNING

If thou must love me, let it be for nought
Except for love's sake only. Do not say
'I love her for her smile...her look...her way
Of speaking gently,...for a trick of thought
That falls in well with mine, and certes brought
A sense of pleasant ease on such a day'—
For these things in themselves, Beloved, may
Be changed, or change for thee,—and love, so wrought
May be unwrought so. Neither love me for
Thine own dear pity's wiping my cheek dry,—
A creature might forget to weep, who bore
Thy comfort long, and lose thy love thereby!
But love me for love's sake, that evermore
Thou mayst love on, through love's eternity.

To My Mistress in Absence

THOMAS CAREW

Though I must live here, and by force
Of your command suffer divorce;
Though I am parted, yet my mind,
That's more myself, still stays behind.
I breathe in you, you keep my heart;
Twas but a carcass that did part.
Then though our bodies are disjoined,
As things that are to place confined,
Yet let our boundless spirits meet,
And in love's sphere each other greet;
There let us work a mystic wreath,
Unknown unto the world beneath;
There let our clasped loves sweetly twin,
There let our secret thoughts unseen
Like nets be weaved and intertwined,
Where with we'll catch each other's mind.
There whilst our souls do sit and kiss,
Tasting a sweet and subtle bliss
Such as gross lovers cannot know,
Whose hands and lips meet here below,
Let us look down, and mark what pain
Our absent bodies here sustain,
And smile to see how far away
The one doth from the other stray;

Yet burn and languish with desire
To join, and quench their mutual fire.
There let us joy to see from far
Our emulous flames at loving war,
Whilst both with equal lustre shine,
Mine bright as yours, yours bright as mine.
There seated in those heavenly bowers,
We'll cheat the lag and lingering hours,
Making our bitter absence sweet,
Till souls and bodies both may meet.

Song of Solomon 2:1-14

I am the rose of Sharon, and the lily of the valleys. As the lily among thorns, so is my love among the daughters. As the apple tree among the trees of the wood, so is my beloved among the sons. I sat down under his shadow with great delight, and his fruit was sweet to my taste. He brought me to the banqueting house, and his banner over me was love. Stay me with flagons, comfort me with apples: for I am sick of love. His left hand is under my head, and his right hand doth embrace me. I charge you, O ye daughters of Jerusalem, by the roes, and by the hinds of the field, that ye stir not up, nor awake my love, till he please. The voice of my beloved! behold, he cometh leaping upon the mountains, skipping upon the hills. My beloved is like a roe or a young hart: behold, he standeth behind our wall, he looketh forth at the windows, shewing himself through the lattice. My beloved spake, and said unto me, Rise up, my love, my fair one, and come away. For, lo, the winter is past, the rain is over and gone; The flowers appear on the earth; the time of the singing of birds is come, and the voice of the turtle is heard in our land; The fig tree putteth forth her green figs, and the vines with the tender grape give a good smell. Arise, my love, my fair one, and come away. O my dove, that art in the clefts of the rock, in the secret places of the stairs, let me see thy countenance, let me hear thy voice; for sweet is thy voice, and thy countenance is comely.

Sonnet 116

WILLIAM SHAKESPEARE

Let me not to the marriage of true minds
Admit impediments; love is not love
Which alters when it alteration finds,
Or bends with the remover to remove:
O, no, it is an ever-fixed mark,
That looks on tempests and is never shaken;
It is the star to every wand'ring bark,
Whose worth's unknown, although his height be taken.
Love's not Time's fool, though rosy lips and cheeks
Within his bending sickle's compass come;
Love alters not with his brief hours and weeks,
But bears it out even to the edge of doom.
If this be error and upon my proved,
I never writ, nor no man ever loved.

That Time of Year Thou Mayst in Me Behold

WILLIAM SHAKESPEARE

That time of year thou mayst in me behold
When yellow leaves, or none, or few, do hang
Upon those boughs which shake against the cold,
Bare ruin'd choirs, where late the sweet birds sang.
In me thou seest the twilight of such day
As after sunset fadeth in the west,
Which by and by black night doth take away,
Death's second self, that seals up all in rest.
In me thou seest the glowing of such fire,
That on the ashes of his youth doth lie,
As the deathbed whereon it must expire,
Consum'd with that which it was nourish'd by.
This thou perceiv'st, which makes thy love more strong,
To love that well which thou must leave ere long.

There Is a Lady Sweet and Kind

THOMAS FORD

There is a lady sweet and kind,
Was never face so pleased my mind;
I did but see her passing by,
And yet I love her till I die.

Her gesture, motion and her smiles,
Her wit, her voice, my heart beguiles,
Beguiles my heart, I know not why,
And yet I love her till I die.

Had I her fast betwixt mine arms,
Judge you that think such sports were harms,
Were't any harm? No, no, fie, fie!
For I will love her till I die.

Cupid is wingéd and doth range;
Her country so my love doth change,
But change she earth, or change she sky,
Yet will I love her till I die.

Though I Am Young and Cannot Tell

BEN JONSON

Though I am young, and cannot tell
  Either what Death or Love is well,
Yet I have heard they both bear darts,
  And both do aim at human hearts.
And then again, I have been told
  Love wounds with heat, as Death with cold;
So that I fear they do but bring
  Extremes to touch, and mean one thing.

As in a ruin we it call
  One thing to be blown up, or fall;
Or to our end like way may have
  By a flash of lightning, or a wave;
So Love's inflaméd shaft or brand
  May kill as soon as Death's cold hand;
Except Love's fires the virtue have
  To fright the frost out of the grave.

Song: Love Lives Beyond the Tomb

JOHN CLARE

Love lives beyond
The tomb, the earth, which fades like dew—
   I love the fond,
The faithful, and the true.

Love lives in sleep,
'Tis happiness of healthy dreams,
   Eve's dews may weep,
But love delightful seems.

'Tis seen in flowers,
And in the even's pearly dew
   On earth's green hours,
And in the heaven's eternal blue.

'Tis heard in spring
When light and sunbeams, warm and kind,
   On angel's wing
Brings love and music to the wind.

And where's the voice
So young, so beautiful, and sweet
   As nature's choice,
Where spring and lovers meet?

Love lives beyond
The tomb, the earth, the flowers, and dew.
I love the fond,
The faithful, young, and true.

Remember

CHRISTINA ROSSETTI

Remember me when I am gone away,
  Gone far away into the silent land;
  When you can no more hold me by the hand,
Nor I half turn to go yet turning stay.
Remember me when no more day by day
  You tell me of our future that you planned:
  Only remember me; you understand
It will be late to counsel then or pray.
Yet if you should forget me for a while
  And afterwards remember, do not grieve:
  For if the darkness and corruption leave
  A vestige of the thoughts that once I had,
Better by far you should forget and smile
  Than that you should remember and be sad.

Echo

CHRISTINA ROSSETTI

Come to me in the silence of the night;
  Come in the speaking silence of a dream;
Come with soft rounded cheeks and eyes as bright
  As sunlight on a stream;
    Come back in tears,
O memory, hope, love of finished years.

Oh dream how sweet, too sweet, too bitter sweet,
  Whose wakening should have been in Paradise,
Where souls brimful of love abide and meet;
  Where thirsting longing eyes
    Watch the slow door
That opening, letting in, lets out no more.

Yet come to me in dreams, that I may live
  My very life again tho' cold in death:
Come back to me in dreams, that I may give
  Pulse for pulse, breath for breath:
    Speak low, lean low,
As long ago, my love, how long ago.

Pining for Far-Off Love

To Lucasta, Going Beyond the Seas

RICHARD LOVELACE

If to be absent were to be
Away from thee;
Or that when I am gone,
You or I were alone;
Then, my Lucasta, might I crave
Pity from blustering wind or swallowing wave.

But I'll not sigh one blast or gale
To swell my sail,
Or pay a tear to 'suage
The foaming blue god's rage;
For whether he will let me pass
Or no, I'm still as happy as I was.

Though seas and land be twixt us both,
Our faith and troth,
Like separated souls,
All time and space controls;
Above the highest sphere we meet
Unseen, unknown, and greet as Angels greet.

So then we do anticipate
Our after-fate,
And are alive in the skies,
If thus our lips and eyes
Can speak like spirits unconfined
In Heaven, their earthy bodies left behind.

Sonnets from the Portuguese XLIV

ELIZABETH BARRETT BROWNING

Belovèd, thou hast brought me many flowers
Plucked in the garden, all the summer through
And winter, and it seemed as if they grew
In this close room, nor missed the sun and showers.
So, in the like name of that love of ours,
Take back these thoughts which here unfolded too,
And which on warm and cold days I withdrew
From my heart's ground. Indeed, those beds and bowers
Be overgrown with bitter weeds and rue,
And wait thy weeding; yet here's eglantine,
Here's ivy!—take them, as I used to do
Thy flowers, and keep them where they shall not pine.
Instruct thine eyes to keep their colours true,
And tell thy soul, their roots are left in mine.

She Was a Phantom of Delight

WILLIAM WORDSWORTH

She was a phantom of delight
When first she gleamed upon my sight;
A lovely apparition, sent
To be a moment's ornament;
Her eyes as stars of twilight fair;
Like Twilight's, too, her dusky hair;
But all things else about her drawn
From May-time and the cheerful dawn;
A dancing shape, an image gay,
To haunt, to startle, and waylay.

I saw her upon nearer view,
A spirit, yet a woman too!
Her household motions light and free,
And steps of virgin-liberty;
A countenance in which did meet
Sweet records, promises as sweet;
A creature not too bright or good
For human nature's daily food,
For transient sorrows, simple wiles,
Praise, blame, love, kisses, tears, and smiles.

And now I see with eye serene
The very pulse of the machine;
A being breathing thoughtful breath,
A traveller between life and death:
The reason firm, the temperate will,
Endurance, foresight, strength, and skill;
A perfect woman, nobly planned
To warn, to comfort, and command;
And yet a spirit still, and bright
With something of an angel-light.

The Flower's Name

ROBERT BROWNING

Here's the garden she walked across,
Arm in my arm, such a short while since:
Hark! now I push its wicket, the moss
Hinders the hinges, and makes them wince.
She must have reached this shrub ere she turned,
As back with that murmur the wicket swung;
For she laid the poor snail my chance foot spurned,
To feed and forget it the leaves among.

Down this side of the gravel walk
She went while her robe's edge brushed the box;
And here she paused in her gracious talk
To point me a moth on the milk-white phlox.
Roses, ranged in valiant row,
I will never think that she passed you by!
She loves you, noble roses, I know;
But yonder see where the rock-plants lie!

This flower she stopped at, finger on lip,–
Stooped over, in doubt, as settling its claim;
Till she gave me, with pride to make no slip,
Its soft meandering Spanish name.

What a name! was it love or praise?
Speech half asleep, or song half awake?
I must learn Spanish one of these days,
Only for that slow sweet name's sake.

Roses, if I live and do well,
I may bring her one of these days,
To fix you fast with as fine a spell,—
Fit you each with his Spanish phrase.
But do not detain me now, for she lingers
There, like sunshine over the ground;
And ever I see her soft white fingers
Searching after the bud she found.

Flower, you Spaniard! look that you grow not,—
Stay as you are, and be loved forever.
Bud, if I kiss you, 't is that you blow not,—
Mind! the shut pink mouth opens never!
For while thus it pouts, her fingers wrestle,
Twinkling the audacious leaves between,
Till round they turn, and down they nestle:
Is not the dear mark still to be seen?

Where I find her not, beauties vanish;
Whither I follow her, beauties flee.
Is there no method to tell her in Spanish
June's twice June since she breathed it with me?

Come, bud! show me the least of her traces.
Treasure my lady's lightest footfall:
Ah! you may flout and turn up your faces,–
Roses, you are not so fair after all!

Sonnet 29

WILLIAM SHAKESPEARE

When, in disgrace with Fortune and men's eyes,
I all alone beweep my outcast state,
And trouble deaf heaven with my bootless cries,
And look upon myself and curse my fate,
Wishing me like to one more rich in hope,
Featured like him, like him with friends possessed,
Desiring this man's art and that man's scope,
With what I most enjoy contented least;
Yet in these thoughts myself almost despising,
Haply I think on thee, and then my state
(Like to the lark at break of day arising
From sullen earth) sings hymns at heaven's gate;
For thy sweet love remembered such wealth brings
That then I scorn to change my state with kings.

When We Two Parted

GEORGE GORDON, LORD BYRON

When we two parted
  In silence and tears,
Half broken-hearted
  To sever for years,
Pale grew thy cheek and cold,
  Colder thy kiss;
Truly that hour foretold
  Sorrow to this.

The dew of the morning
  Sunk chill on my brow–
It felt like the warning
  Of what I feel now.
Thy vows are all broken,
  and light is thy fame;
I hear thy name spoken,
  And share in its shame.

They name thee before me,
  A knell to mine ear;
A shudder comes o'er me–
  Why were thou so dear?
They know not I knew thee,
  Who knew thee too well–

Long, long shall I rue thee,
  Too deeply to tell.

In secret we met–
  In silence I grieve,
That thy heart could forget,
  Thy spirit deceive.
If I should meet thee
  After long years,
How should I greet thee?–
  With silence and tears.

Song of Solomon 3:1-4

By night on my bed I sought him whom my soul loveth: I sought him, but I found him not. I will rise now, and go about the city in the streets, and in the broad ways I will seek him whom my soul loveth: I sought him, but I found him not. The watchmen that go about the city found me: to whom I said, Saw ye him whom my soul loveth? It was but a little that I passed from them, but I found him whom my soul loveth: I held him, and would not let him go.

What Is Love

Sonnet 18

WILLIAM SHAKESPEARE

Shall I compare thee to a summer's day?
Thou art more lovely and more temperate:
Rough winds do shake the darling buds of May,
And summer's lease hath all too short a date:
Sometime too hot the eye of heaven shines
And often is his gold complexion dimmed;
And every fair from fair sometimes declines,
By chance or nature's changing course untrimmed;
But thy eternal summer shall not fade,
Nor lose possession of that fair thou ow'st,
Nor shall death brag though wander'st in his shade,
When in eternal lines to time thou grow'st:
So long as men can breathe, or eyes can see,
So long lives this, and this gives life to thee.

The Clod and the Pebble

WILLIAM BLAKE

"Love seeketh not Itself to please,
Nor for itself hath any care;
But for another gives its ease,
And builds a Heaven in Hell's despair."

So sang a little Clod of Clay,
Trodden with the cattle's feet;
But a Pebble of the brook,
Warbled out these metres meet:

"Love seeketh only Self to please,
To bind another to Its delight:
Joys in another's loss of ease,
And builds a Hell in Heaven's despite."

Yet Is Their Hope: Then Love But Play Thy Part

MARY WROTH

Yet is their hope: Then Love but play thy part
Remember well thy self, and think on me;
Shine in those eyes which conquer'd have my heart;
And see if mine be slack to answer thee:
Lodge in that breast, and pity moving see
For flames which in mine burn in truest smart
Exiling thoughts that touch inconstancy,
Or those which waste not in the constant art,
Watch but my sleep, if I take any rest
For thought of you, my spirit so distressed
As pale, and famish'd, I, for mercy cry;
Will you your servant leave? Think but on this;
Who wears love's crown, must not do so amiss,
But seek their good, who on thy force do lie.

Sonnet 130

WILLIAM SHAKESPEARE

My mistress' eyes are nothing like the sun;
Coral is far more red than her lips' red;
If snow be white, why then her breasts are dun;
If hairs be wires, black wires grow on her head.
I have seen roses damasked, red and white,
But no such roses see I in her cheeks;
And in some perfumes is there more delight
Than in the breath that from my mistress reeks.
I love to hear her speak, yet well I know
That music hath a far more pleasing sound;
I grant I never saw a goddess go;
My mistress, when she walks, treads on the ground.
And yet, by heaven, I think my love as rare
As any she belied with false compare.

Oh Mistress Mine

WILLIAM SHAKESPEARE

Oh mistress mine! where are you roaming?
Oh! stay and hear; your true love's coming,
  That can sing both high and low.
Trip no further, pretty sweeting;
Journeys end in lovers meeting,
  Every wise man's son doth know.

What is love? 'tis not hereafter;
Present mirth hath present laughter;
  What's to come is still unsure:
In delay there lies no plenty;
Then come kiss me, sweet and twenty,
  Youth's a stuff will not endure.

Love's Growth

JOHN DONNE

I scarce believe my love to be so pure
   As I had thought it was,
   Because it doth endure
Vicissitude, and season, as the grass;
Methinks I lied all winter, when I swore
My love was infinite, if spring make' it more.

But if this medicine, love, which cures all sorrow
With more, not only be no quíntessence,
But mixed of all stuffs paining soul or sense,
And of the sun his working vigor borrow,
Love's not so pure, and abstract, as they use
To say, which have no mistress but their muse,
But as all else, being elemented too,
Love sometimes would contémplate, sometimes do.

And yet no greater, but more eminent,
   Love by the spring is grown;
   As, in the firmament,
Stars by the sun are not enlarged, but show,
Gentle love deeds, as blossoms on a bough,
From love's awakened root do bud out now.

If, as in water stirred more circles be
Produced by one, love such additions take,
Those, like so many spheres, but one heaven make,
for they are all concentric unto thee;
And though each spring do add to love new heat,
As princes do in times of action get
New taxes, and remit them not in peace,
No winter shall abate the spring's increase.

The Definition of Love

ANDREW MARVELL

My Love is of a birth as rare
As 'tis, for object, strange and high;
It was begotten by Despair
Upon Impossibility.

Magnanimous Despair alone
Could show me so divine a thing,
Where feeble Hope could ne'er have flown
But vainly flapped its tinsel wing.

And yet I quickly might arrive
Where my extended soul is fixed;
But Fate does iron wedges drive,
And always crowds itself betwixt.

For Fate with jealous eye does see
Two perfect loves, nor lets them close;
Their union would her ruin be,
And her tyrannic power depose.

And therefore her decrees of steel
Us as the distant poles have placed
(Though Love's whole world on us doth wheel),
Not by themselves to be embraced,

Unless the giddy heaven fall,
And earth some new convulsion tear,
And, us to join, the world should all
Be cramped into a planisphere.

As lines, so loves oblique may well
Themselves in every angle greet;
But ours, so truly parallel,
Though infinite, can never meet.

Therefore the love which us doth bind,
But Fate so enviously debars,
Is the conjunction of the mind,
And opposition of the stars.

I Corinthians 13:1-13

Though I speak with the tongues of men and of angels, and have not charity, I am become as sounding brass, or a tinkling cymbal. And though I have the gift of prophecy, and understand all mysteries, and all knowledge; and though I have all faith, so that I could remove mountains, and have not charity, I am nothing. And though I bestow all my goods to feed the poor, and though I give my body to be burned, and have not charity, it profiteth me nothing. Charity suffereth long, and is kind; charity envieth not; charity vaunteth not itself, is not puffed up, Doth not behave itself unseemly, seeketh not her own, is not easily provoked, thinketh no evil; Rejoiceth not in iniquity, but rejoiceth in the truth; Beareth all things, believeth all things, hopeth all things, endureth all things. Charity never faileth: but whether there be prophecies, they shall fail; whether there be tongues, they shall cease; whether there be knowledge, it shall vanish away. For we know in part, and we prophesy in part. But when that which is perfect is come, then that which is in part shall be done away. When I was a child, I spake as a child, I understood as a child, I thought as a child: but when I became a man, I put away childish things. For now we see through a glass, darkly; but then face to face: now I know in part; but then shall I know even as also I am known. And now abideth faith, hope, charity, these three; but the greatest of these is charity.

The Bonds
of Love

Sonnets from the Portuguese XXIX

ELIZABETH BARRETT BROWNING

I think of thee! my thoughts do twine and bud
About thee, as wild vines, about a tree,
Put out broad leaves, and soon there's nought to see
Except the straggling green which hides the wood.
Yet, O my palm-tree, be it understood
I will not have my thoughts instead of thee
Who art dearer, better! Rather, instantly
Renew thy presence; as a strong tree should,
Rustle thy boughs and set thy trunk all bare,
And let these bands of greenery which insphere thee
Drop heavily down, burst, shattered, everywhere!
Because, in this deep joy to see and hear thee
And breathe within thy shadow a new air,
I do not think of thee—I am too near thee.

Never the Time and the Place

ROBERT BROWNING

Never the time and the place
And the loved one all together!
This path—how soft to pace!
This May—what magic weather!
Where is the loved one's face?
In a dream that loved one's face meets mine,
But the house is narrow, the place is bleak
Where, outside, rain and wind combine
With a furtive ear, if I strive to speak,
With a hostile eye at my flushing cheek,
With a malice that marks each word, each sign!
O enemy sly and serpentine,
Uncoil thee from the waking man!
Do I hold the Past
Thus firm and fast
Yet doubt if the Future hold I can?
This path so soft to pace shall lead
Thro' the magic of May to herself indeed!
Or narrow if needs the house must be,
Outside are the storms and strangers: we
Oh, close, safe, warm sleep I and she,—
I and she!

To Anthea, Who May Command Him Any Thing

ROBERT HERRICK

Bid me to live, and I will live
Thy Protestant to be;
Or bid me to love, and I will give
A loving heart to thee.

A heart as soft, a heart as kind,
A heart as sound and free
As in the whole world thou canst find,
That heart I'll give to thee.

Bid me to weep, and I will weep
While I have eyes to see:
And, having none, yet I will keep
A heart to weep for thee.

Bid me despair, and I'll despair
Under that cypress tree:
Or bid me die, and I will dare
E'en death to die for thee.

Thou art my life, my love, my heart
The very eyes of me:
And hast command of every part
To live and die for thee.

The Passionate Shepherd to His Love

CHRISTOPHER MARLOWE

Come live with me and be my love,
And we will all the pleasures prove
That valleys, grooves, hills, fields,
Woods, or steepy mountain yields.

And we will sit upon the rocks,
Seeing the shepherds feed their flocks
By shallow rivers, to whose falls
Melodious birds sing madrigals.

And I will make thee beds of roses
And a thousand fragrant posies;
A cap of flowers, and a kirtle
Embroidered all with leaves of myrtle.

A gown made of the finest wool
Which from our pretty lambs we pull;
Fair-lined slippers for the cold,
With buckles of the purest gold;

A belt of straw and ivy buds
With coral clasps and amber studs:
And if these pleasures may thee move,
Come live with me and be my love.

The shepherd swains shall dance and sing
For thy delight each May morning:
If these delights thy mind may move,
Then live with me and be my love.

Sonnets from the Portuguese XLIII

ELIZABETH BARRETT BROWNING

How do I love thee? Let me count the ways.
I love thee to the depth and breadth and height
My soul can reach, when feeling out of sight
For the ends of Being and ideal Grace.
I love thee to the level of everyday's
Most quiet need, by sun and candle-light.
I love thee freely, as men strive for Right;
I love thee purely, as they turn from Praise.
I love thee with the passion put to use
In my old griefs, and with my childhood's faith.
I love thee with a love I seemed to lose
With my lost saints,—I love thee with the breath,
Smiles, tears, of all my life!—and, if God choose,
I shall but love thee better after death.

Sonnets from the Portuguese XXXVIII

ELIZABETH BARRETT BROWNING

First time he kissed me, he but only kissed
The fingers of this hand wherewith I write;
And ever since, it grew more clean and white,
Slow to world-greetings, quick with its "Oh, list,"
When the angels speak. A ring of amethyst
I could not wear here, plainer to my sight,
Than that first kiss. The second passed in height
The first, and sought the forehead, and half missed,
Half falling on the hair. O beyond meed!
That was the chrism of love, which love's own crown,
With sanctifying sweetness, did precede.
The third upon my lips was folded down
In perfect, purple state; since when, indeed,
I have been proud and said, "My love, my own."

Sonnets from the Portuguese XXXV

ELIZABETH BARRETT BROWNING

If I leave all for thee, wilt thou exchange
And be all to me? Shall I never miss
Home-talk and blessing and the common kiss
That comes to each in turn, nor count it strange
When I look up, to drop on a new range
Of walls and floors, another home than this?
Nay, wilt thou fill that place by me which is
Filled by dead eyes too tender to know change?
That's hardest. If to conquer love, has tried,
To conquer grief, tries more, as all things prove;
For grief indeed is love and grief beside.
Alas, I have grieved so I am hard to love.
Yet love me—wilt thou? Open thine heart wide,
And fold within the wet wings of thy dove.

Answer to a Child's Question

SAMUEL TAYLOR COLERIDGE

Do you ask what the birds say? The sparrow, the dove,
The linnet, and thrush say "I love, and I love!"
In the winter they're silent, the wind is so strong;
What it says I don't know, but it sings a loud song.
But green leaves, and blossoms, and sunny warm
    weather,
And singing and loving—all come back together.
But the lark is so brimful of gladness and love,
The green fields below him, the blue sky above,
That he sings, and he sings, and forever sings he,
"I love my Love, and my Love loves me."

From Paradise Lost
Adam to Eve

JOHN MILTON

O fairest of creation, last and best
Of all God's works, creature in whom excelled
Whatever can to sight or thought be formed,
Holy, divine, good, amiable, or sweet!
How art thou lost, how on a sudden lost,
Defaced, deflowered, and now to death devote!
Rather, how hast thou yielded to transgress
The strict forbiddance, how to violate.
The sacred fruit forbidden! Some cursed fraud
Of enemy hath beguiled thee, yet unknown,
And me with thee hath ruined, for with thee
Certain my resolution is to die.
How can I live without thee, how forego
Thy sweet converse, and love so dearly joined,
To live again in these wild woods forlorn?
Should God create another Eve, and I
Another rib afford, yet loss of thee
Would never from my heart; no, no, I feel
The link of nature draw me: flesh of flesh,
Bone of my bone thou art, and from thy state
Mine never shall be parted, bliss or woe.

However, I with thee have fixed my lot,
Certain to undergo like doom; if death
Consort with thee, death is to me as life;
So forcible within my heart I feel
The bond of nature draw me to my own,
My own in thee, for what thou art is mine;
Our state cannot be severed, we are one,
One flesh; to lose thee were to lose myself.

Give All to Love

RALPH WALDO EMERSON

Give all to love;
Obey thy heart;
Friends, kindred, days,
Estate, good-frame,
Plans, credit, and the Muse,–
Nothing refuse.

'Tis a brave master;
Let it have scope:
Follow it utterly,
Hope beyond hope:
High and more high
It dives into noon,
With wing unspent,
Untold intent;
But it is a god,
Knows its own path,
And the outlets of the sky.

It was not for the mean;
It requireth courage stout,
Souls above doubt,
Valor unbending;
It will reward,–

They shall return
More than they were,
And ever ascending.

Leave all for love;
Yet, hear me, yet,
One word more thy heart behoved,
One pulse more of firm endeavor,—
Keep thee today,
To-morrow, forever,
Free as an Arab
Of thy beloved.

Cling with life to the maid;
But when the surprise,
First vague shadow of surmise
Flits across her bosom young
Of a joy apart from thee
Free be she, fancy-free;
Nor thou detain her vesture's hem,
Nor the palest rose she flung
From her summer diadem.

From Monna Innominata

CHRISTINA ROSSETTI

I wish I could remember that first day,
First hour, first moment of your meeting me,
If bright or dim the season, it might be
Summer or winter for aught I can say;
So unrecorded did it slip away,
So blind was I to see and to foresee,
So dull to mark the budding of my tree
That would not blossom yet for many a May.
If only I could recollect it, such
A day of days! I let it come and go
As traceless as a thaw of bygone snow;
It seemed to mean so little, meant so much;
If only now I could recall that touch,
First touch of hand in hand—Did one but know!

The Sun Rising

JOHN DONNE

Busy old fool, unruly sun,
Why dost thou thus,
Through windows, and through curtains, call on us?
Must to thy motions lovers' seasons run?
Saucy pedantic wretch, go chide
Late schoolboys, and sour prentices,
Go tell court-huntsmen that the King will ride,
Call country ants to harvest offices;
Love, all alike, no season knows, nor clime,
Nor hours, days, months, which are the rags of time.

Thy beams, so reverend and strong
Why shouldst thou think?
I could eclipse and cloud them with a wink,
But that I would not lose her sight so long:
If her eyes have not blinded thine,
Look, and tomorrow late, tell me
Whether both the Indias of spice and mine
Be where thou leftst them, or lie here with me.
Ask for those kings whom thou saw'st yesterday,
And thou shalt hear: "All here in one bed lay."

The Flea

JOHN DONNE

Mark but this flea, and mark in this
How little that which thou deny'st me is;
It sucked me first, and now sucks thee,
And in this flea our bloods mingled be;
Thou know'st that this cannot be said
A sin, nor shame, nor loss of maidenhead,
Yet this enjoys before it woo,
And pampered swells with one blood made of two,
And this, alas, is more than we would do.

Oh stay, three lives in one flea spare,
Where we almost, yea more than married are.
This flea is you and I, and this
Our marriage bed, and marriage temple is;
Though parents grudge, and you, we're met
And cloistered in these living walls of jet.
Though use make you apt to kill me,
Let not to that, self-murder added be,
And sacrilege, three sins in killing three.

Cruel and sudden, hast thou since
Purpled they nail in blood of innocence?
Wherein could this flea guilty be,
Except in that drop which it sucked from thee?

Yet thou triumph'st, and say'st that thou
Find'st not thyself, nor me, the weaker now;
'Tis true; then learn how false, fears be;
Just so much honor, when thou yield'st to me,
Will waste, as this flea's death took life from thee.

Dover Beach

MATTHEW ARNOLD

The sea is calm tonight.
The tide is full, the moon lies fair
Upon the straits–on the French coast the light
Gleams and is gone; the cliffs of England stand,
Glimmering and vast, out in the tranquil bay.
Come to the window, sweet is the night air!
Only, from the long line of spray
Where the sea meets the moon-blanched land,
Listen! you hear the grating roar
Of pebbles which the waves draw back, and fling,
At their return, up the high strand,
Begin, and cease and then again begin,
With tremulous cadence slow, and bring
The eternal note of sadness in.

Sophocles long ago
Heard it on the Aegean, and it brought
Into his mind the turbid ebb and flow
Of human misery; we
Find also in the sound a thought,
Hearing it by this distant northern sea.

The Sea of Faith
Was once, too, at the full, and round earth's shore

Lay like the folds of a bright girdle furled.
But now I only hear
Its melancholy, long, withdrawing roar,
Retreating, to the breath
Of the night wind, down the vast edges drear
And naked shingles of the world.

Ah, love, let us be true
To one another! for the world, which seems
To lie before us like a land of dreams,
So various, so beautiful, so new,
Hath really neither joy, nor love, nor light,
Nor certitude, nor peace, nor help for pain;
And we are here as on a darkling plain
Swept with confused alarms of struggle and flight,
Where ignorant armies clash by night.

The Unquiet Grave

ANONYMOUS

1

"The wind doth blow today, my love,
  And a few small drops of rain;
I never had but one true-love,
  In cold grave she was lain.

2

"I'll do as much for my true-love
  As any young man may;
I'll sit and mourn all at her grave
  For a twelvemonth and a day."

3

The twelvemonth and a day being up,
  The dead began to speak:
"Oh who sits weeping on my grave,
  And will not let me sleep?"

4

"'T is I, my love, sits on your grave,
  And will not let you sleep;
For I crave one kiss of your clay-cold lips,
  And that is all I seek."

5

"You crave one kiss of my clay-cold lips,
  But my breath smells earthy strong;
If you have one kiss of my clay-cold lips,

Your time will not be long.

   6

"'T is down in yonder garden green,
  Love, where we used to walk,
The finest flower that e'er was seen
  Is withered to a stalk.

   7

"The stalk is withered dry, my love,
  So will our hearts decay;
So make yourself content, my love,
  Till God calls you away."

When I Peruse the Conquer'd Fame

WALT WHITMAN

When I peruse the conquer'd fame of heroes and the
  victories of mighty generals, I do not envy the
  generals,
Nor the President in his Presidency, nor the rich in his
  great house,
But when I hear of the brotherhood of lovers, how it was
  with them,
How together through life, through dangers, odium,
  unchanging, long and long,
Through youth and through middle and old age, how
  unfaltering, how affectionate and faithful they were,
Then I am pensive—I hastily walk away fill'd with the
  bitterest envy.

The Fair Singer

ANDREW MARVELL

To make a final conquest of all me,
Love did compose so sweet an enemy,
In whom both beauties to my death agree,
Joining themselves in fatal harmony;
That while she with her eyes my heart does bind,
She with her voice might captivate my mind.

I could have fled from one but singly fair:
My disentangled soul itself might save,
Breaking the curléd trammels of her hair.
But how should I avoid to be her slave,
Whose subtle art invisibly can wreathe
My fetters of the very air I breathe?

It had been easy fighting in some plain,
Where victory might hang in equal choice,
But all resistance against her is vain,
Who has th' advantage both of eyes and voice,
And all my forces needs must be undone,
She having gainéd both the wind and sun.

Soul-Love

Somewhere

Sir Edwin Arnold

Somewhere there waiteth in this world of ours
For one lone soul, another lonely soul—
Each chasing each through all the weary hours,
And meeting strangely at one sudden goal;
Then blend they—like green leaves with golden
    flowers,
Into one beautiful and perfect whole—
And life's long night is ended, and the way
Lies open onward to eternal day.

The Good-Morrow

JOHN DONNE

I wonder, by my troth, what thou and I
Did till we loved. Were we not weaned till then,
But sucked on country pleasures, childishly?
Or snorted we in the seven sleepers' den?
'Twas so; but this, all pleasures fancies be.
If ever any beauty I did see,
Which I desired and got, 'twas but a dream of thee.

And now good-morrow to our waking souls,
Which watch not one another out of fear
For love all love of other sights controls
And makes one little room an everywhere.
Let sea-discoverers to new worlds have gone,
Let maps to others worlds on worlds have shown,
Let us possess one world, each hath one, and is one.

My face in thine eye, thine in mine appears,
And true plain hearts do in the faces rest
Where can we find two better hemispheres
Without sharp North, without declining West?
Whatever dies was not mixed equally;
If our two loves be one, or thou and I
Love so alike that none do slacken, none can die.

Sonnets from the Portuguese XXXIX

ELIZABETH BARRETT BROWNING

Because thou hast the power and own'st the grace
To look through and behind this mask of me
(Against which years have beat thus blanchingly
With their rains), and behold my soul's true face,
The dim and weary witness of life's race,—
Because thou hast the faith and love to see,
Through that same soul's distracting lethargy,
The patient angel waiting for a place
In the new Heavens,—because nor sin nor woe,
Nor God's infliction, nor death's neighbourhood,
Nor all which others viewing, turn to go,
Nor all which makes me tired of all, self-viewed,—
Nothing repels thee,...Dearest, teach me so
To pour out gratitude, as thou dost, good!

Sonnets from the Portuguese XXI

ELIZABETH BARRETT BROWNING

Say over again, and yet once over "again,"
That thou dost love me. Though the word repeated
Should seem 'a cuckoo-song,' as thou dost treat it,
Remember, never to the hill or plain,
Valley and wood, without her cuckoo-strain,
Comes the fresh Spring in all her green completed.
Belovèd, I, amid the darkness greeted
By a doubtful spirit-voice, in that doubt's pain
Cry, 'Speak once more—thou lovest!' Who can fear
Too many stars, though each in heaven shall roll—
Too many flowers, though each shall crown the year?
Say thou dost love me, love me, love me—toll
The silver iterance!—only minding, Dear,
To love me also in silence, with thy soul.

Asia

Percy Bysshe Shelley

My soul is an enchanted boat,
Which, like a sleeping swan, doth float
Upon the silver waves of thy sweet singing;
And thine doth like an angel sit
Beside a helm conducting it,
Whilst all the winds with melody are ringing.
It seems to float ever, forever,
Upon that many-winding river,
Between mountains, woods, abysses,
A paradise of wildernesses!
Till, like one in slumber bound,
Borne to the ocean, I float down, around,
Into a sea profound, of ever-spreading sound:

Meanwhile thy spirit lifts its pinions
In music's most serene dominions;
Catching the winds that fan that happy heaven.
And we sail on, away, afar,
Without a course, without a star,
But, by the instinct of sweet music driven;
Till through Elysian garden islets
By thee, most beautiful of pilots,
Where never mortal pinnace glided,
The boat of my desire is guided:

Realms where the air we breathe is love,
Which in the winds and on the waves doth move,
Harmonizing this earth with what we feel above.

Meeting at Night

ROBERT BROWNING

The grey sea and the long black land;
And the yellow half-moon large and low;
And the startled little waves that leap
In fiery ringlets from their sleep,
As I gain the cove with pushing prow,
And quench its speed i' the slushy sand.

Then a mile of warm sea-scented beach;
Three fields to cross till a farm appears;
A tap at the pane, the quick sharp scratch
And blue spurt of a lighted match,
And a voice less loud, through its joys and fears,
Than the two hearts beating each to each!

303

EMILY DICKINSON

The Soul selects her own Society—
Then—shuts the Door—
To her divine Majority—
Present no more—

Unmoved—she notes the Chariots—pausing—
At her low Gate—
Unmoved—an Emperor be kneeling
Upon her Mat—

I've known her—from an ample nation—
Choose One—
Then—close the Valve of her attention—
Like Stone—

Surprised by Joy

WILLIAM WORDSWORTH

Surprised by joy—impatient as the Wind
I turned to share the transport—Oh! with whom
But thee, deep buried in the silent tomb,
That spot which no vicissitude can find?
Love, faithful love, recalled thee to my mind—
But how could I forget thee? Through what power,
Even for the least division of an hour,
Have I been so beguiled as to be blind
To my most grievous loss!—That thought's return
Was the worst pang that sorrow ever bore,
Save one, one only, when I stood forlorn,
Knowing my heart's best treasure was no more;
That neither present time, nor years unborn
Could to my sight that heavenly face restore.

True Beauty

From Endymion: Book I

JOHN KEATS

A thing of beauty is a joy for ever:
Its loveliness increases; it will never
Pass into nothingness; but still will keep
A bower quiet for us, and a sleep
Full of sweet dreams, and health, and quiet breathing.
Therefore, on every morrow, are we wreathing
A flowery band to bind us to the earth,
Spite of despondence, of the inhuman dearth
Of noble natures, of the gloomy days,
Of all the unhealthy and o'er-darkened ways
Made for our searching: yes, in spite of all,
Some shape of beauty moves away the pall
From our dark spirits. Such the sun, the moon,
Trees old and young, sprouting a shady boon
For simple sheep; and such are daffodils
With the green world they live in; and clear rills
That for themselves a cooling covert make
'Gainst the hot season; the mid forest brake,
Rich with a sprinkling of fair musk-rose blooms:
And such too is the grandeur of the dooms
We have imagined for the mighty dead;
All lovely tales that we have heard or read:
An endless fountain of immortal drink,
Pouring unto us from the heaven's brink.

Amoretti
Sonnet LXXIX: Men Call You Fair

EDMUND SPENSER

Men call you fair, and you do credit it,
For that yourself ye daily such do see:
But the true fair, that is the gentle wit
And virtuous mind, is much more praised of me:
For all the rest, however fair it be,
Shall turn to naught and lose that glorious hue;
But only that is permanent and free
From frail corruption that doth flesh ensue.
That is true beauty; that doth argue you
To be divine, and born of heavenly seed;
Derived from that fair Spirit from whom all true
And perfect beauty did at first proceed:
  He only fair, and what he fair hath made;
  All other fair, like flowers, untimely fade.

Let Beauty Awake

ROBERT LOUIS STEVENSON

Let Beauty awake in the morn from beautiful dreams,
   Beauty awake from rest!
   Let Beauty awake
   For Beauty's sake
In the hour when the birds awake in the brake
   And the stars are bright in the west!

Let Beauty awake in the eve from the slumber of day,
   Awake in the crimson eve!
   In the day's dusk end
   When the shades ascend,
Let her wake to the kiss of a tender friend
   To render again and receive!

I Am

JOHN CLARE

I am: yet what I am none cares or knows
My friends forsake me like a memory lost,
I am the self-consumer of my woes—
They rise and vanish in oblivious host,
Like shadows in love's frenzied stifled throes
And yet I am, and live—like vapors tossed

Into the nothingness of scorn and noise,
Into the living sea of waking dreams,
Where there is neither sense of life or joys,
But the vast shipwreck of my life's esteems;
Even the dearest, that I love the best,
And strange—nay, rather strange than the rest.

I long for scenes where man has never trod,
A place where woman never smile or wept—
There to abide with my creator, God,
And sleep as I in childhood sweetly slept,
Untroubling and untroubled where I lie,
The grass below—above the vaulted sky.

The Divine Image

WILLIAM BLAKE

To Mercy, Pity, Peace, and Love,
All pray in their distress:
And to these virtues of delight
Return their thankfulness.

For Mercy, Pity, Peace, and Love,
Is God our father dear:
And Mercy, Pity, Peace, and Love,
Is Man his child and care.

For Mercy has a human heart
Pity, a human face:
And Love, the human form divine,
And Peace, the human dress.

Then every man of every clime,
That prays in his distress,
Prays to the human form divine
Love, Mercy, Pity, Peace.

And all must love the human form,
In heathen, Turk or Jew.
Where Mercy, Love, and Pity dwell,
There God is dwelling too.

Hymn

EDGAR ALLAN POE

At morn—at noon—at twilight dim—
Maria! thou hast heard my hymn!
In joy and woe—in good and ill—
Mother of God, be with me still!
When the hours flew brightly by,
And not a cloud obscured the sky,
My soul, lest it should truant be,
Thy grace did guide to thine and thee;
Now, when storms of Fate o'ercast
Darkly my Present and my Past,
Let my Future radiant shine
With sweet hopes of thee and thine!

She Walks in Beauty

George Gordon, Lord Byron

1

She walks in beauty, like the night
  Of cloudless climes and starry skies;
And all that's best of dark and bright
  Meet in her aspect and her eyes:
Thus mellowed to that tender light
  Which heaven to gaudy day denies.

2

One shade the more, one ray the less,
  Had half impaired the nameless grace
Which waves in every raven tress,
  Or softly lightens o'er her face;
Where thoughts serenely sweet express
  How pure, how dear their dwelling place.

3

And on that cheek, and o'er that brow,
  So soft, so calm, yet eloquent,
The smiles that win, the tints that glow,
  But tell of days in goodness spent,
A mind at peace with all below,
  A heart whose love is innocent!

449

EMILY DICKINSON

I died for Beauty—but was scarce
Adjusted in the Tomb
When One who died for Truth, was lain
In an adjoining Room—

He questioned softly "Why I failed"?
"For Beauty", I replied—
"And I—for Truth—Themself are One—
We Brethren, are", He said—

And so, as Kinsmen, met a Night—
We talked between the Rooms—
Until the Moss had reached our lips—
And covered up—our names—

In Praise
of Beauty

Song to Celia

BEN JONSON

Drink to me only with thine eyes,
And I will pledge with mine;
Or leave a kiss but in the cup,
And I'll not look for wine.
The thirst that from the soul doth rise
Doth ask a drink divine:
But might I of Jove's nectar sup,
I would not change for thine.
I sent thee, late, a rosy wreath,
Not so much honoring thee,
As giving it a hope that there
It could not withered be.
But thou thereon did'st only breathe,
And sent'st it back to me;
Since when it grows, and smells, I swear,
Not of itself, but thee.

Upon Julia's Clothes

ROBERT HERRICK

When as in silks my Julia goes,
Then, then, me thinks, how sweetly flows
That liquefaction of her clothes.
Next, when I cast mine eyes and see
That brave vibration each way free;
O, how that glittering taketh me!

There Is a Garden in Her Face

THOMAS CAMPION

There is a garden in her face
Where roses and white lilies grow;
A heavenly paradise is that place
Wherein all pleasant fruits do flow.
There cherries grow which none may buy
Till "Cherry-ripe" themselves do cry.

Those cherries fairly do enclose
Of orient pearl a double row,
Which when her lovely laughter shows,
They look like rose-buds filled with snow;
Yet them nor peer prince can buy,
Till "Cherry-ripe" themselves do cry.

Her eyes like angels watch them still;
Her brows like bended bows do stand,
Threatening with piercing frowns to kill
All that attempt, with eye or hand
Those sacred cherries to come nigh
Till "Cherry-ripe" themselves do cry.

Love

SAMUEL TAYLOR COLERIDGE

All thoughts, all passions, all delights,
Whatever stirs this mortal frame,
All are but ministers of Love,
And feed his sacred flame.

Oft in my waking dreams do I
Live o'er again that happy hour,
When midway on the mount I lay,
Beside the ruined tower.

The moonshine, stealing o'er the scene
Had blended with the lights of eve;
And she was there, my hope, my joy,
My own dear Genevieve!

Ode on a Grecian Urn

John Keats

Thou still unravished bride of quietness,
Thou foster-child of silence and slow time,
Sylvan historian, who canst thus express
A flowery tale more sweetly than our rhyme:
What leaf-fringed legend haunts about thy shape
Of deities or mortals, or of both.
In Tempe or the dales of Arcady?
What men or gods are these? what maidens loth?
What made pursuit? What struggle to escape?
What pipes and timbrels? What wild ecstasy?

Heard melodies are sweet, but those unheard
Are sweeter; therefore, ye soft pipes, play on;
Not to the sensual ear, but, more endeared,
Pipe to the spirit ditties of no tone:
Fair youth, beneath the trees, thou canst not leave
Thy song, nor ever can those trees be bare;
Bold Lover, never, never canst thou kiss,
Though winning near the goal—yet, do not grieve;
She cannot fade, though thou hast not thy bliss,
For ever wilt thou love, and she be fair!

Ah, happy, happy boughs! that cannot shed
Your leaves, nor ever bid the Spring adieu;
And, happy melodist, unwearied,
For ever piping songs for ever new;
More happy love! more happy, happy love!
For ever warm and still to be enjoyed,
For ever panting, and for ever young;
All breathing human passion far above,
That leaves a heart high-sorrowful and cloyed,
A burning forehead, and a parching tongue.

Who are these coming to the sacrifice?
To what green altar, O mysterious priest,
Lead'st thou that heifer lowing at the skies,
And all her silken flanks with garlands drest?
What little town by river or sea shore,
Or mountain-built with peaceful citadel,
Is emptied of this folk, this pious morn?
And, little town, thy streets for evermore
Will silent be; and not a soul to tell
Why thou art desolate, can e'er return.

O Attic shape! Fair attitude! with brede
Of marble men and maidens overwrought,
With forest branches and the trodden weed;
Thou, silent form, dost tease us out of thought
As doth eternity: Cold Pastoral!

When old age shall this generation waste,
Thou shalt remain, in midst of other woe
Than ours, a friend to man, to whom thou say'st,
"Beauty is truth, truth beauty—that is all
Ye know on earth, and all ye need to know."

In an Artist's Studio

CHRISTINA ROSSETTI

One face looks out from all his canvases,
One selfsame figure sits or walks or leans;
We found her hidden just behind those screens,
That mirror gave back all her loveliness.
A queen in opal or in ruby dress,
A nameless girl in freshest summer-greens,
A saint, an angel;—every canvass means
The same one meaning, neither more nor less.
He feeds upon her face by day and night,
And she with true kind eyes looks back on him
Fair as the moon and joyful as the light:
Not wan with waiting, not with sorrow dim;
Not as she is, but was when hope shone bright;
Not as she is, but as she fills his dream.

Love for Nature

Thanatopsis

WILLIAM CULLEN BRYANT

To him who, in the love of Nature, holds
Communion with her visible forms, she speaks
A various language: for his gayer hours
She has a voice of gladness, and a smile
And eloquence of beauty; and she glides
Into his darker musings, with a mild
And healing sympathy, that steals away
Their sharpness, ere he is aware. When thoughts
Of the last bitter hour come like a blight
Over thy spirit, and sad images
Of the stern agony, and shroud, and pall,
And breathless darkness, and the narrow house
Make thee to shudder, and grow sick at heart,
Go forth under the open sky, and list
To Nature's teachings, while from all around.

My Star

ROBERT BROWNING

All that I know
Of a certain star,
Is, it can throw
(Like the angled spar)
Now a dart of red,
Now a dart of blue,
Till my friends have said
They would fain see, too,
My star that dartles the red and the blue!

Then it stops like a bird; like a flower, hangs furled:
They must solace themselves with the Saturn above it.
What matter to me if their star is a world?
Mine has opened its soul to me; therefore I love it.

Song from the Ship

THOMAS LOVELL BEDDOES

To sea, to sea! The calm is o'er;
The wanton water leaps in sport,
And rattles down the pebbly shore;
The dolphin wheels, the sea-cows snort,
And unseen Mermaids' pearly song
Comes bubbling up, the weeds among.
Fling broad the sail, dip deep the oar:
To sea, to sea! the calm is o'er.

To sea, to sea! our wide-winged bark
Shall billowy cleave its sunny way,
And with its shadow, fleet and dark,
Break the caved Tritons' azure day,
Like mighty eagle soaring light
O'er antelopes on Alpine height.
The anchor heaves, the ship swings free,
The sails swell full. To sea, to sea!

Psalm 147: 4-5, 14-18

He telleth the number of the stars; he calleth them all by their names. Great is our Lord, and of great power: his understanding is infinite. He maketh peace in thy borders, and filleth thee with the finest of the wheat. He sendeth forth his commandment upon earth: his word runneth very swiftly. He giveth snow like wool: he scattereth the hoarfrost like ashes. He casteth forth his ice like morsels: who can stand before his cold? He sendeth out his word, and melteth them: he causeth his wind to blow, and the waters flow.

Dying Speech of an Old Philosopher

WALTER SAVAGE LANDOR

I strove with none, for none was worth my strife:
  Nature I loved, and, next to Nature, Art:
I warmed both hands before the fire of Life;
  It sinks; and I am ready to depart.

God's Grandeur

GERARD MANLEY HOPKINS

The world is charged with the grandeur of God.
  It will flame out, like shining from shook foil;
  It gathers to a greatness, like the ooze of oil
Crushed. Why do men then now not reck his rod?
Generations have trod, have trod, have trod;
  And all is seared with trade; bleared, smeared
    with toil;
  And wears man's smudge and shares man's smell:
    the soil
Is bare now, nor can foot feel, being shod.

And for all this, nature is never spent;
  There lives the dearest freshness deep down things;
And though the last lights off the black West went
  Oh, morning, at the brown brink eastward, springs—
Because the Holy Ghost over the bent
  World broods with warm breast and with ah! bright
    wings.

441

EMILY DICKINSON

This is my letter to the World
That never wrote to Me—
The simple News that Nature told—
With tender Majesty

Her Message is committed
To Hands I cannot see—
For love of her—Sweet—countrymen—
Judge tenderly—of Me

The Beauty of Nature

737

EMILY DICKINSON

The Moon was but a Chin of Gold
A Night or two ago—
And now she turns Her perfect Face
Upon the World below—

Her Forehead is of Amplest Blonde—
Her Cheek—a Beryl hewn—
Her Eye unto the Summer Dew
The likest I have known—

Her Lips of Amber never part—
But what must be the smile
Upon Her Friend she would confer
Were such Her Silver Will—

And what a privilege to be
But the remotest Star—
For Certainty She take Her Way
Beside Your Palace Door—

Her Bonnet is the Firmament—
The Universe—Her Shoe—
The Stars—the Trinkets at Her Belt—
Her Dimities—of Blue—

It Is a Beauteous Evening

WILLIAM WORDSWORTH

It is a beauteous evening, calm and free,
The holy time is quiet as a Nun
Breathless with adoration; the broad sun
Is sinking down in its tranquillity;
The gentleness of heaven broods o'er the Sea;
Listen! the mighty Being is awake,
And doth with his eternal motion make
A sound like thunder—everlastingly.

The Eagle: A Fragment

ALFRED, LORD TENNYSON

He clasps the crag with crooked hands;
Close to the sun in lonely lands,
Ringed with the azure world, he stands.

The wrinkled sea beneath him crawls;
He watches from his mountain walls,
And like a thunderbolt he falls.

I Wandered Lonely as a Cloud

WILLIAM WORDSWORTH

I wandered lonely as a cloud
That floats on high o'er vales and hills,
When all at once I saw a crowd,
A host, of golden daffodils;
Beside the lake, beneath the trees,
Fluttering and dancing in the breeze.

Continuous as the stars that shine
And twinkle on the milky way,
They stretched in never-ending line
Along the margin of a bay:
Ten thousand saw I at a glance,
Tossing their heads in sprightly dance.

The waves beside them danced; but they
Out-did the sparkling waves in glee:
A poet could not but be gay,
In such a jocund company:
I gazed—and gazed—but little thought
What wealth the show to me had brought:

For oft, when on my couch I lie
In vacant or in pensive mood,
They flash upon that inward eye

Which is the bliss of solitude;
And then my heart with pleasure fills,
And dances with the daffodils.

On the Uniformity and Perfection of Nature

PHILIP FENEAU

Who looks through nature with an eye
That would the scheme of heaven descry,
Observes her constant, still the same,
In all her laws, through all her frame.

No imperfection can be found
In all that is, above, around,—
All, nature made, in reason's sight
Is order all, and all is right.

From In Memoriam A. H. H. Epilogue

ALFRED, LORD TENNYSON

And rise, O moon, from yonder down,
Till over down and over dale
All night the shining vapor sail
And pass the silent-lighted town,

The white-faced halls, the glancing rills,
And catch at every mountain head,
And o'er the friths that branch and spread
Their sleeping silver thro' the hills;

And touch with shade the bridal doors,
With tender gloom the roof, the wall;
And breaking let the splendor fall
To spangle all the happy shores

By which they rest, and ocean sounds,
And, star and system rolling past,
A soul shall draw from out the vast
And strike his being into bounds,

And, moved thro' life of lower phase,
Result in man, be born and think,
And act and love, a closer link
Betwixt us and the crowning race

Of those that, eye to eye, shall look
On knowledge; under whose command
Is Earth and Earth's, and in their hand
Is Nature like an open book;

No longer half-akin to brute,
For all we thought and loved and did,
And hoped, and suffer'd, is but seed
Of what in them is flower and fruit;

Wereof the man that with me trod
This planet was a noble type
Appearing ere the times were ripe,
That friend of mine who lives in God,

That God, which ever lives and loves,
One God, one law, one element,
And one far-off divine event,
To which the whole creation moves.

Follow Thy Fair Sun

THOMAS CAMPION

Follow thy fair sun, unhappy shadow;
Though thou be black as night,
And she made all of light,
Yet follow thy fair sun, unhappy shadow.

Follow her whose light thy light depriveth;
Though here thou liv'st disgraced,
And she in heaven is placed,
Yet follow her whose light the world reviveth!

Follow those pure beams whose beauty burneth,
That so have scorched thee,
As thou still black must be,
Till her kind beams thy black to brightness turneth.

Follow her while yet her glory shineth;
There comes a luckless night,
That will dim all her light;
And this the black unhappy shade divineth.

Follow still since so thy fates ordained;
The sun must have his shade,
Till both at once do fade;
The sun still proved, the shadow still disdained.

To the Evening Star

WILLIAM BLAKE

Thou fair-hair'd angel of the evening,
Now, while the sun rests on the mountains, light
Thy bright torch of love; thy radiant crown
Put on, and smile upon our evening bed!
Smile on our loves; and, while thou drawest the
Blue curtains of the sky, scatter thy silver dew
On every flower that shuts its sweet eyes
In timely sleep. Let thy west wind sleep on
The lake; speak silence with thy glimmering eyes,
And wash the dusk with silver. Soon, full soon,
Dost thou withdraw; then the wolf rages wide,
And the lion glares thro' the dun forest:
The fleeces of our flocks are cover'd with
Thy sacred dew: protect them with thine influence.

Delighting
in Nature

Song

Percy Bysshe Shelley

V

I love all that thou loves,
Spirit of Delight!
The fresh Earth in new leaves dressed,
And the starry night;
Autumn evening, and the morn
When the golden mists are born.

VI

I love snow, and all the forms
Of the radiant frost;
I love waves, and winds and storms,
Everything almost
Which is Nature's, and may be
Untainted by man's misery.

VII

I love tranquil solitude,
And such society
As is quiet, wise, and good;
Between thee and me
What difference? but thou dost possess
The things I seek, not love them less.

VIII

I love Love—though he has wings,
And like light can flee,
But above all other things,
Spirit, I love thee—
Thou art love and life! Oh, come,
Make once more my heart thy home.

328

EMILY DICKINSON

A Bird came down the Walk—
He did not know I saw—
He bit an Angleworm in halves
And ate the fellow, raw,

And then he drank a Dew
From a convenient Grass—
And then hopped sidewise to the Wall
To let a Beetle pass—

He glanced with rapid eyes
That hurried all around—
They looked like frightened Beads, I thought—
He stirred his Velvet Head

Like one in danger, Cautious,
I offered him a Crumb
And he unrolled his feathers
And rowed him softer home—

Than Oars divide the Ocean,
Too silver for a seam—
Or Butterflies, off Banks of Noon
Leap, splashless as they swim.

Aftermath

HENRY WADSWORTH LONGFELLOW

When the summer fields are mown,
When the birds are fledged and flown,
And the dry leaves strew the path:
With the falling of the snow,
With the cawing of the crow,
Once again the fields we mow
And gather in the aftermath.

Not the sweet, new grass with flowers
Is this harvesting of ours;
Not the upland clover bloom;
But the rowen mixed with weeds,
Tangled tufts from marsh and meads,
Where the poppy drops its seeds
In the silence and the gloom.

The Yellow Violet

WILLIAM CULLEN BRYANT

When beechen buds begin to swell,
And woods the blue-bird's warble know,
The yellow violet's modest bell
Peeps from the last year's leaves below.

Ere russet fields their green resume,
Sweet flower, I love, in forest bare,
To meet thee, when thy faint perfume
Alone is in the virgin air.

Of all her train, the hands of Spring
First plant thee in the watery mould,
And I have seen thee blossoming
Beside the snow-bank's edges cold.

Thy parent sun, who bade thee view
Pale skies, and chilling moisture sip,
Has bathed thee in his own bright hue,
And streaked with jet thy glowing lip.

Yet slight thy form, and low thy seat,
And earthward bent thy gentle eye,
Unapt the passing view to meet,
When loftier flowers are flaunting nigh.

Oft, in the sunless April day,
Thy early smile has stayed my walk;
But midst the gorgeous blooms of May,
I passed thee on thy humble stalk.

So they, who climb to wealth, forget
The friends in darker fortunes tried.
I copied them—but I regret
That I should ape the ways of pride.

And when again the genial hour
Awakes the painted tribes of light.
I'll not o'erlook the modest flower
That made the woods of April bright.

Job 38:6-12, 24-28; 41:33

Whereupon are the foundations thereof fastened? or who laid the corner stone thereof; When the morning stars sang together, and all the sons of God shouted for joy? Or who shut up the sea with doors, when it brake forth, as if it had issued out of the womb? When I made the cloud the garment thereof, and thick darkness a swaddlingband for it, And brake up for it my decreed place and set bars and doors, And said, Hitherto shalt thou come, but no further: and here shall thy proud waves be stayed? Hast thou commanded the morning since thy days; and caused the dayspring to know his place?... By what way is the light parted, which scattereth the east wind upon the earth? Who hath divided a watercourse for the overflowing of waters, or a way for the lightning of thunder; To cause it to rain on the earth where no man is; on the wilderness, wherein there is no man; To satisfy the desolate and waste ground; and to cause the bud of the tender herb to spring forth? Hath the rain a father? or who hath begotten the drops of dew?... Upon earth there is not his like, who is made without fear.

Seasons

With a Flower

EMILY DICKINSON

When roses cease to bloom, dear,
And violets are done,
When bumble-bees in solemn flight
Have passed beyond the sun,

The hand that paused to gather
Upon this summer's day
Will idle lie, in Auburn,
Then take my flower, pray!

The Autumn

ELIZABETH BARRETT BROWNING

Go, sit upon the lofty hill,
And turn your eyes around,
Where waving woods and waters wild
Do hymn an autumn sound.
The summer sun is faint on them
The summer flowers depart
Sit still as all transform'd to stone,
Except your musing heart.

How there you sat in summer-time,
May yet be in your mind;
And how you heard the green woods sing
Beneath the freshening wind.
Though the same wind now blows around,
You would its blast recall;
For every breath that stirs the trees,
Doth cause a leaf to fall.

Oh! like that wind, is all the mirth
That flesh and dust impart:
We cannot bear its visitings,
When change is on the heart.

Gay words and jests may make us smile,
When Sorrow is asleep;
But other things must make us smile,
When Sorrow bids us weep!

The dearest hands that clasp our hands,
Their presence may be o'er;
The dearest voice that meets our ear,
That tone may come no more!
Youth fades; and then, the joys of youth,
Which once refresh'd our mind,
Shall come as, on those sighing woods,
The chilling autumn wind.

Hear not the wind view not the woods;
Look out o'er vale and hill
In spring, the sky encircled them
The sky is round them still.
Come autumn's scathe come winter's cold
Come change and human fate!
Whatever prospect Heaven doth bound,
Can ne'er be desolate.

The Spring

THOMAS CAREW

Now that the winter's gone, the earth hath lost
Her snow-white robes, and now no more the frost
Candies the grass, or casts an icy cream
Upon the silver lake or crystal stream;
But the warm sun thaws the benumbed earth,
And makes it tender; gives a sacred birth
To the dead swallow; wakes in hollow tree
The drowsy cuckoo and the humble-bee.
Now do a choir of chirping minstrels bring
In triumph to the world the youthful spring.
The valleys, hills, and woods in rich array
Welcome the coming of the longed-for May.

Mutability

PERCY BYSSHE SHELLEY

1
The flower that smiles today
  Tomorrow dies;
All that we wish to stay,
  Tempts and then flies.
What is this world's delight?
Lightning that mocks the night,
  Brief even as bright.

2
Virtue, how frail it is!
  Friendship how rare!
Love, how it sells poor bliss
  For proud despair!
But we, though soon they fall,
Survive their joy and all
  Which ours we call.

3
Whilst skies are blue and bright,
  Whilst flowers are gay,
Whilst eyes that change ere night
  Make glad the day,
Whilst yet the calm hours creep,
Dream thou—and from thy sleep
  Then wake to weep.

Snowflakes

HENRY WADSWORTH LONGFELLOW

Out of the bosom of the Air,
  Out of the cloud-folds of her garments shaken,
Over the woodlands brown and bare,
  Over the harvest-fields forsaken,
    Silent, and soft, and slow
    Descends the snow.

Even as our cloudy fancies take
  Suddenly shape in some divine expression,
Even as the troubled heart doth make
  In the white countenance confession,
    The troubled sky reveals
    The grief it feels.

This is the poem of the air,
  Slowly in silent syllables recorded;
This is the secret of despair,
  Long in its cloudy bosom hoarded,
    Now whispered and revealed
    To wood and field.

Character

Speak Gently

DAVID BATES

Speak gently! It is better far
To rule by love, than fear
Speak gently let not harsh words mar
The good we might do here!

Speak gently! Love doth whisper low
The vows that true hearts bind;
And gently Friendship's accents flow;
Affection's voice is kind.

Speak gently to the little child!
Its love be sure to gain;
Teach it in accents soft and mild:
It may not long remain.

Speak gently to the young, for they
Will have enough to bear
Pass through this life as best they may,
'T is full of anxious care!

Speak gently to the aged one,
Grieve not the care-worn heart;
The sands of life are nearly run,
Let such in peace depart!

Speak gently, kindly, to the poor;
Let no harsh tone be heard;
They have enough they must endure,
Without an unkind word!

Speak gently to the erring—know,
They may have toiled in vain;
Perchance unkindness made them so;
Oh, win them back again!

Speak gently! He who gave his life
To bend man's stubborn will,
When elements were in fierce strife,
Said to them, "Peace, be still."

Speak gently! 't is a little thing
Dropped in the heart's deep well;
The good, the joy, which it may bring,
Eternity shall tell.

Song by an Old Shepherd

WILLIAM BLAKE

When silver snow decks Sylvio's clothes,
And jewel hangs at shepherd's nose,
We can abide life's pelting storm,
That makes our limbs quake, if our hearts be warm.

Whilst Virtue is our walking-staff,
And Truth a lantern to our path,
We can abide life's pelting storm,
That makes our limbs quake, if our hearts be warm.

Blow, boisterous wind, stern winter frown,
Innocence is a winter's gown.
So clad, we'll abide life's pelting storm,
That makes our limbs quake, if our hearts be warm.

Patient Grissill

THOMAS DEKKER

Art thou poor, yet hast thou golden slumbers?
O sweet content!
Art thou rich, yet is thy mind perplexed?
O punishment!
Dost thou laugh to see how fools are vexed
To add to golden numbers, golden numbers?
O sweet content! O sweet, O sweet content!
Work apace, apace, apace, apace;
Honest labour bears a lovely face;
Then hey nonny nonny, hey nonny nonny!

Canst drink the waters of the crisped spring?
O sweet content!
Swimm'st thou in wealth, yet sink'st in thine
     own tears?
O punishment!
Then he that patiently want's burden bears
No burden bears, but is a king, a king:
O sweet content! O sweet, O sweet content!
Work apace, apace, apace, apace;
Honest labour bears a lovely face;
Then hey nonny nonny, hey nonny nonny!

An Essay on Criticism

ALEXANDER POPE

Of all the causes which conspire to blind
Man's erring judgment, and misguide the mind,
What the weak head with strongest bias rules,
Is pride, the never-failing vice of fools.
Whatever Nature has in worth denied,
She gives in large recruits of needful pride;
For as in bodies, thus in souls, we find
What wants in blood and spirits swelled with wind:
Pride, where wit fails, steps in to our defense,
And fills up all the mighty void of sense.
If once right reason drives that cloud away,
Truth breaks upon us with resistless day.
Trust not yourself: but your defects to know,
Make use of every friend—every foe.

Virtue

GEORGE HERBERT

Sweet day, so cool, so calm, so bright,
  The bridal of the earth and sky:
The dew shall weep thy fall tonight;
      For thou must die.

Sweet rose, whose hue, angry and brave,
  Bids the rash gazer wipe his eye:
Thy root is ever in its grave,
      And thou must die.

Sweet spring, full of sweet days and roses,
  A box where sweets compacted lie;
My music shows ye have your closes,
      And all must die.

Only a sweet and virtuous soul,
  Like seasoned timber, never gives;
But though the whole world turn to coal,
      Then chiefly lives.

Death and Eternity

Nature

HENRY WADSWORTH LONGFELLOW

As a fond mother, when the day is o'er,
Leads by the hand her little child to bed,
Half willing, half reluctant to be led,
And leave his broken playthings on the floor,
Still gazing at them through the open door,
Nor wholly reassured and comforted
By promises of others in their stead,
Which, though more splendid, may not please him more:
So Nature deals with us, and takes away
Our playthings one by one, and by the hand
Leads us to rest so gently, that we go
Scarce knowing if we wish to go or stay,
Being too full of sleep to understand
How far the unknown transcends the what we know.

The First Snowfall

EMILY DICKINSON

The snow had begun in the gloaming,
And busily all the night
Had been heaping field and highway
With a silence deep and white.

Every pine and fir and hemlock
Wore ermine too dear for an earl,
And the poorest twig on the elm-tree
Was ridged inch deep with pearl.

From sheds new-roofed with Carrara
Came Chanticleer's muffled crow,
The stiff rails were softened to swan's-down,
And still fluttered down the snow.

I stood and watched by the window
The noiseless work of the sky,
And the sudden flurries of snow-birds,
Like brown leaves whirling by.

I thought of a mound in sweet Auburn
Where a little headstone stood;
How the flakes were folding it gently,
As did robins the babes in the wood.

Up spoke our own little Mabel,
Saying, "Father, who makes it snow?"
And I told of the good All-father
Who cares for us here below.

Again I looked at the snow-fall,
And thought of the leaden sky
That arched o'er our first great sorrow,
When that mound was heaped so high.

I remember the gradual patience
That fell from that cloud-like snow,
Flake by flake, healing and hiding
The scar of our deep-plunged woe.

And again to the child I whispered,
"The snow that husheth all,
Darling, the merciful Father
Alone can make it fall!"

Then, with eyes that saw not, I kissed her;
And she, kissing back, could not know
That my kiss was given to her sister,
Folded close under deepening snow.

Sonnets from the Portuguese XLII

Elizabeth Barrett Browning

"My future will not copy fair my past"—
I wrote that once; and thinking at my side
My ministering life-angel justified
The word by his appealing look upcast
To the white throne of God, I turned at last,
And there, instead, saw thee, not unallied
To angels in thy soul! Then I, long tried
By natural ills, received the comfort fast,
While budding, at thy sight, my pilgrim's staff
Gave out green leaves with morning dews imperiled.
I seek no copy now of life's first half:
Leave here the pages with long musing curled,
And write me new my future's epigraph,
New angel mine, unhoped for in the world!

Before This Little Gift Was Come

ROBERT LOUIS STEVENSON

Before this little gift was come
The little owner had made haste for home;
And from the door of where the eternal dwell,
Looked back on human things and smiled farewell.
O may this grief remain the only one!
O may our house be still a garrison
Of smiling children, and for evermore
The tune of little feet be heard along the floor!

From Holy Sonnets
10

JOHN DONNE

Death, be not proud, though some have called thee
Mighty and dreadful, for thou art not so;
For those whom thou think'st thou dost overthrow
Die not, poor Death, nor yet canst thou kill me.
From rest and sleep, which but thy pictures be,
Much pleasure; then from thee much more must flow,
And soonest our best men with thee do go,
Rest of their bones, and soul's delivery.
Thou art slave to fate, chance, kings, and desperate men,
And dost with poison, war, and sickness dwell,
And poppy or charms can make us sleep as well
And better than thy stroke; why swell'st thou then?
One short sleep past, we wake eternally
And death shall be no more, Death, thou shalt die.

On My First Son

BEN JONSON

Farewell, thou child of my right hand, and joy;
My sin was too much hope of thee, loved boy.
Seven years thou wert lent to me, and I thee pay,
Exacted by thy fate, on the just day.
O, could I lose all father now! For why
Will man lament the state he should envy?
To have so soon 'scaped world's and flesh's rage,
And, if no other misery, yet age?
Rest in soft peace, and asked, say, "Here doth lie
Ben Jonson his best piece of poetry."
For whose sake, henceforth, all his vows be such
As what he loves may never like too much.

XLI

ELIZABETH BARRETT BROWNING

I thank all who have loved me in their hearts,
With thanks and love from mine. Deep thanks to all
Who paused a little near the prison-wall
To hear my music in its louder parts
Ere they went onward, each one to the mart's
Or temple's occupation, beyond call.
But thou, who, in my voice's sink and fall,
When the sob took it, thy divinest Art's
Own instrument didst drop down at thy foot
To hearken what I said between my tears,—
Instruct me how to thank thee! Oh, to shoot
My soul's full meaning into future years,
That they should lend it utterance, and salute
Love that endures, from Life that disappears!

A Reminiscence

ANNE BRONTË

Yes, thou art gone! and never more
Thy sunny smile shall gladden me;
But I may pass the old church door,
And pace the floor that covers thee.

May stand upon the cold, damp stone,
And think that, frozen, lies below
The lightest heart that I have known,
The kindest I shall ever know.

Yet, though I cannot see thee more,
'Tis still a comfort to have seen;
And though thy transient life is o'er,
'Tis sweet to think that thou hast been;

To think a soul so near divine,
Within a form so angel fair,
United to a heart like thine,
Has gladdened once our humble sphere.

From Song of Myself
6

WALT WHITMAN

A child said *What is the grass?* fetching it to me with full
    hands;
How could I answer the child? I do not know what it is
    any more than he.

I guess it must be the flag of my disposition, out of
    hopeful green stuff woven.

Or I guess it is the handkerchief of the Lord,
A scented gift and remembrancer designedly dropt,
Bearing the owner's name someway in the corners,
    that we may see and remark, and say *Whose?*

Or I guess the grass is itself a child, the produced babe
    of the vegetation.

Or I guess it is a uniform hieroglyphic,
And it means, Sprouting alike in broad zones and
    narrow zones,
Growing among black folks as among white,
Kanuck, Tuckahoe, Congressman, Cuff, I give them the
    same, I receive them the same.

And now it seems to me the beautiful uncut hair of
  graves.

Tenderly will I use you curling grass,
It may be you transpire from the breasts of young men,
It may be if I had known them I would have loved them,
It may be you are from old people, or from offspring
  taken soon out of their mothers' laps,
And here you are the mothers' laps.

This grass if very dark to be from the white heads of
  old mothers,
Darker than the colorless beards of old men,
Dark to come from under the faint red roofs of
  mouths.

O I perceive after all so many uttering tongues,
And I perceive they do not come from the roofs of
  mouths for nothing.

I wish I could translate the hints about the dead young
  men and women,
And the hints about old men and mothers, and the offspring taken soon out of their laps.

What do you think has become of the young and old
  men?

And what do you think has become of the women and
   children?

They are alive and well somewhere,
The smallest sprout shows there is really no death,
And if ever there was it led forward life, and does not
   wait at the end to arrest it,
And ceas'd the moment life appear'd.

All goes onward and outward, nothing collapses,
And to die is different from what any one supposed,
   and luckier.

712

EMILY DICKINSON

Because I could not stop for Death—
He kindly stopped for me—
The Carriage held but just Ourselves—
And Immortality

We slowly drove—He knew no haste
And I had put away
My labor and my leisure too,
For His Civility—

We passed the School, where Children strove
At Recess—in the Ring—
We passed the Fields of Gazing Grain—
We passed the Setting Sun—

Or rather—He passed Us—
The Dews drew quivering and chill—
For only Gossamer, my Gown—
My Tippet—only Tulle—

We paused before a House that seemed
A Swelling of the Ground—
The Roof was scarcely visible—
The Cornice—in the Ground—

Since then—'tis Centuries—and yet
Feels shorter than the Day
I first surmised the Horses' Heads
Were toward Eternity—

Life and Death

CHRISTINA ROSSETTI

Life is not sweet. One day it will be sweet
To shut our eyes and die:
Nor feel the wild flowers blow, nor birds dart by
With flitting butterfly,
Nor grass grow long above our heads and feet,
Nor hear the happy lark that soars sky high,
Nor sigh that spring is fleet and summer fleet,
Nor mark the waxing wheat,
Nor know who sits in our accustomed seat.

Life is not good. One day it will be good
To die, then live again;
To sleep meanwhile: so not to feel the wane
Of shrunk leaves dropping in the wood,
Nor hear the foamy lashing of the main,
Nor mark the blackened bean-fields, nor where stood
Rich ranks of golden grain
Only dead refuse stubble clothe the plain:
Asleep from risk, asleep from pain.

The Silver Swan

ORLANDO GIBBONS

The silver swan, who living had no note,
When death approached, unlocked her silent throat;
Leaning her breast against the reedy shore,
Thus sung her first and last, and sung no more:
"Farewell, all joys; Oh death, come close mine eyes;
More geese than swans now live, more fools than
  wise."

Sonnet 146

WILLIAM SHAKESPEARE

Poor soul, the center of my sinful earth,
Lord of these rebel powers that thee array,
Why dost thou pine within and suffer dearth,
Painting thy outward walls so costly gay?
Why so large cost, having so short a lease,
Dost thou upon thy fading mansion spend?
Shall worms, inheritors of this excess,
Eat up thy charge? Is this thy body's end?
Then, soul, live thou upon thy servant's loss,
And let that pine to aggravate thy store;
Buy terms divine in selling hours of dross;
Within be fed, without be rich no more.
So shalt thou feed on death, that feeds on men,
And death once dead, there's no more dying then.

Song

JOHN DONNE

Sweetest love, I do not go
  For weariness of thee,
Nor in hope the world can show
  A fitter love for me;
    But since that I
Must die at last, 'tis best
To use myself in jest,
  Thus by feigned deaths to die.

Yesternight the sun went hence,
  And yet is here today;
He hath no desire nor sense,
  Nor half so short a way:
    Then fear not me,
But believe that I shall make
Speedier journeys, since I take
  More wings and spurs than he.

O how feeble is man's power,
  That if good fortune fall,
Cannot add another hour,
  Nor a lost hour recall!
    But come bad chance,
And we join to't our strength,

And we teach it art and length,
  Itself o'er us to'advance.

When thou sigh'st, thou sigh'st not wind,
  But sigh'st my soul away;
When thou weep'st, unkindly kind,
  My life's blood doth decay.
    It cannot be
That thou lov'st me, as thou say'st,
If in thine my life thou waste;
  Thou art the best of me.

Let not thy divining heart
  Forethink me any ill;
Destiny may take thy part
  And may thy fears fulfill;
    But think that we
Are but turned aside to sleep;
They who one another keep
  Alive, ne'er parted be.

From Holy Sonnets
1

JOHN DONNE

Thou hast made me, and shall Thy work decay?
Repair me now, for now mine end doth haste;
I run to death, and death meets me as fast,
And all my pleasures are like yesterday.
I dare not move my dim eyes any way,
Despair behind, and death before doth cast
Such terror, and my feeble flesh doth waste
By sin in it, which it towards hell doth weigh.
Only Thou art above, and when towards Thee
By Thy leave I can look, I rise again;
But our old subtle foe so tempteth me
That not one hour myself I can sustain.
Thy grace may wing me to prevent his art,
And Thou like adamant draw mine iron heart.

A Contemplation upon Flowers

HENRY KING

Brave flowers, that I could gallant it like you,
And be as little vain;
You come abroad and make a harmless show,
And to your beds of earth again;
You are not proud, you know your birth,
For your embroidered garments are from earth.

You do obey your months and times, but I
Would have it ever spring;
My fate would know no winter, never die,
Nor think of such a thing;
Oh that I could my bed of earth but view,
And smile and look as cheerfully as you.

Oh teach me to see death and not to fear,
But rather to take truce;
How often have I seen you at a bier,
And there look fresh and spruce;
You fragrant flowers then teach me that my breath
Like yours may sweeten and perfume my death.

Death Stands Above Me, Whispering Low

WALTER SAVAGE LANDOR

Death stands above me, whispering low
 I know not what into my ear:
Of his strange language all I know
 Is, there is not a word of fear.

Winter Heavens

GEORGE MEREDITH

Sharp is the night, but stars with frost alive
Leap off the rim of earth across the dome.
It is a night to make the heavens our home
More than the nest whereto apace we strive.
Lengths down our road each fir-tree seems a hive,
In swarms outrushing from the golden comb.
They waken waves of thoughts that burst to foam:
The living throb in me, the dead revive.
Yon mantle clothes us: there, past mortal breath,
Life glistens on the river of the death.
It folds us, flesh and dust; and have we knelt,
Or never knelt, or eyed as kine the springs
Of radiance, the radiance enrings:
And this is the soul's haven to have felt.

Song

CHRISTINA ROSSETTI

When I am dead, my dearest,
  Sing no sad songs for me;
Plant thou no roses at my head,
Nor shady cypress tree:
Be the green grass above me
  With showers and dewdrops wet;
And if thou wilt, remember,
  And if thou wilt, forget.

I shall not see the shadows,
  I shall not feel the rain;
I shall not hear the nightingale
  Sing on, as if in pain:
And dreaming through the twilight
  That doth not rise nor set,
Haply I may remember,
  And haply may forget.

419

EMILY DICKINSON

We grow accustomed to the Dark—
When Light is put away—
As when the Neighbor holds the Lamp
To witness her Goodbye—

A Moment—We uncertain step
For newness of the night—
Then—fit our Vision to the Dark—
And meet the Road—erect—

And so of larger—Darknesses—
Those Evenings of the Brain—
When not a Moon disclose a sign—
Or Star—come out—within–

The Bravest—grope a little—
And sometimes hit a Tree
Directly in the Forehead—
But as they learn to see—

Either the Darkness alters—
Or something in the sight
Adjusts itself to Midnight—
And Life steps almost straight.

The Passage of Time

My Heart Leaps Up

WILLIAM WORDSWORTH

My heart leaps up when I behold
A rainbow in the sky:
So was it when my life began;
So is it now I am a man;
So be it when I shall grow old,
Or let me die!
And I could wish my days to be
Bound each to each by natural piety.

If You're Ever Going to Love Me

UNKNOWN

If you're ever going to love me love me now,
  while I can know
All the sweet and tender feelings which from real
  affection flow.
Love me now, while I am living; do not wait till
  I am gone
And then chisel it in marble-warm love words on
  ice-cold stone.
If you've dear, sweet thoughts about me, why not
  whisper them to me?
Don't you know 'twould make me happy and as glad
  as glad could be?
If you wait till I am sleeping, ne'er to waken
  here again,
There'll be walls of earth between us and I couldn't
  hear you then.
If you knew someone was thirsting for a drop
  of water sweet
Would you be so slow to bring it? Would you step
  with laggard feet?
There are tender hearts all around us who are thirsting
  for our love;
Why withhold from them what nature makes them
  crave all else above?

I won't need your kind caresses when the grass grows
   o'er my face;
I won't crave your love or kisses in my last low resting
   place.
So, then, if you love me any, if it's but a little bit,
Let me know it now while living; I can own and
   treasure it.

995

EMILY DICKINSON

This was in the White of the Year—
That—was in the Green—
Drifts were as difficult then to think
As Daisies now to be seen—

Looking back is best that is left
Or if it be—before—
Retrospection is Prospect's half,
Sometimes, almost more.

To the Virgins, to Make Much of Time

ROBERT HERRICK

Gather ye rose-buds while ye may,
Old Time is still a-flying;
And this same flower that smiles today,
Tomorrow will be dying.

The glorious lamp of heaven, the sun,
The higher he's a-getting,
The sooner will his race be run,
And nearer he's to setting.

That age is best which is the first,
When youth and blood are warmer;
But being spent, the worse, and worst
Times still succeed the former.

Then be not coy, but use your time,
And while ye may, go marry;
For having lost but once your prime,
You may for ever tarry.

A Psalm of Life

HENRY WADSWORTH LONGFELLOW

Tell me not, in mournful numbers,
Life is but an empty dream!
For the soul is dead that slumbers,
And things are not what they seem.

Life is real! Life is earnest!
And the grave is not its goal;
Dust thou art, to dust returnest,
Was not spoken of the soul.

Not enjoyment, and not sorrow,
Is our destined end or way;
But to act, that each tomorrow
Finds us farther than today.

Lives of great men all remind us
We can make our lives sublime,
And, departing, leave behind us
Footprints on the sands of time;

Footprints, that perhaps another,
Sailing o'er life's solemn main,
A forlorn and shipwrecked brother,
Seeing, shall take heart again.

Let us, then, be up and doing,
With a heart for any fate;
Still achieving, still pursuing,
Learn to labour and to wait.

Ecclesiastes 3:1-8

To every thing there is a season, and a time to every
purpose under the heaven:

A time to be born, and a time to die; a time to plant,
and a time to pluck up that which is planted;

A time to kill, and a time to heal; a time to break
down, and a time to build up;

A time to weep, and a time to laugh; a time to mourn,
and a time to dance;

A time to cast away stones, and a time to gather stones
together; a time to embrace, and a time to refrain
from embracing;

A time to get, and a time to lose; a time to keep, and a
time to cast away;

A time to rend, and a time to sew; a time to keep
silence, and a time to speak;

A time to love, and a time to hate; a time of war, and a
time of peace.

A Dream within a Dream

EDGAR ALLAN POE

Take this kiss upon the brow!
And, in parting from you now,
Thus much let me avow—
You are not wrong, who deem
That my days have been a dream;
Yet if hope has flown away
In a night, or in a day,

In a vision, or in none,
Is it therefore the less gone?
All that we see or seem
Is but a dream within a dream.

I stand amid the roar
Of a surf-tormented shore,
And I hold within my hand
Grains of the golden sand—
How few! yet how they creep
Through my fingers to the deep,
While I weep—while I weep!
O God! can I not grasp
Them with a tighter clasp?
O God! can I not save
One from the pitiless wave?

Is all that we see or seem
But a dream within a dream?

Days

RALPH WALDO EMERSON

Daughters of Time, the hypocritic Days,
Muffled and dumb like barefoot dervishes,
And marching single in an endless file,
Bring diadems and fagots in their hands.
To each they offer gifts after his will,
Bread, kingdoms, stars, and sky that holds them all.
I, in my pleached garden, watched to pomp,
Forgot my morning wishes, hastily
Took a few herbs and apples, and the Day
Turned and departed silent. I, too late,
Under her solemn fillet saw the scorn.

The Last Leaf

OLIVER WENDELL HOLMES

I saw him once before,
As he passed by the door,
And again
The pavement stones resound,
As he totters o'er the ground
With his cane.

They say that in his prime,
Ere the pruning-knife of Time
Cut him down,
Not a better man was found
By the Crier on his round
Through the town.

But now he walks the streets,
And he looks at all he meets
Sad and wan,
And he shakes his feeble head,
That it seems as if he said,
"They are gone."

The mossy marbles rest
On the lips that he has prest
In their bloom,

And the names he loved to hear
Have been carved for many a year
On the tomb.

My grandmamma has said—
Poor old lady, she is dead
Long ago—
That he had a Roman nose,
And his cheek was like a rose
In the snow;

But now his nose is thin,
And it rests upon his chin
Like a staff,
And a crook is in his back,
And a melancholy crack
In his laugh.

I know it is a sin
For me to sit and grin
At him here;
But the old three-cornered hat,
And the breeches, and all that,
Are so queer!

And if I should live to be
The last leaf upon the tree
In the spring,

Let them smile, as I do now,
At the old forsaken bough
Where I cling.

From Maud, Part II

ALFRED, LORD TENNYSON

O that 'twere possible
After long grief and pain
To find the arms of my true love
Round me once again!

When I was wont to meet her
In the silent woody places
By the home that gave me birth,
We stood tranced in long embraces
Mixt with kisses sweeter sweeter
Than anything on earth.

A shadow flits before me,
Not thou, but like to thee:
Ah Christ, that it were possible
For one short hour to see
The souls we loved, that they might tell us
What and where they be.

It leads me forth at evening,
It lightly winds and steals
In a cold white robe before me,
When all my spirit reels
At the shouts, the leagues of lights
And the roaring of the wheels.

Sonnet 30

WILLIAM SHAKESPEARE

When to the sessions of sweet silent thought
I summon up remembrance of things past,
I sigh the lack of many a thing I sought,
And with old woes new wail my dear time's waste:
Then can I drown an eye (unused to flow)
For precious friends hid in death's dateless night,
And weep afresh love's long since canceled woe,
And moan th' expense of many a vanished sight:
Then can I grieve at grievances foregone,
And heavily from woe to woe tell o'er
The sad account of fore-bemoaned moan,
Which I new pay as if not paid before.
But if the while I think on thee, dear friend,
All losses are restored and sorrows end.

Come, My Celia

BEN JONSON

Come, my Celia, let us prove,
While we can, the sports of love;
Time will not be ours forever;
He at length our good will sever.
Spend not then his gifts in vain.
Suns that set may rise again;
But if once we lose this light,
'Tis with us perpetual night.
Why should we defer our joys?
Fame and rumor are but toys.
Cannot we delude the eyes
Of a few poor household spies,
Or his easier ears beguile,
So removéd by our wile?
'Tis no sin love's fruit to steal;
But the sweet thefts to reveal,
To be taken, to be seen,
These have crimes accounted been.

To Daffodils

ROBERT HERRICK

Fair daffodils, we weep to see
   You haste away so soon:
As yet the early-rising sun
   Has not attained his noon.
      Stay, stay,
   Until the hasting day
      Has run
   But to the evensong;
And, having prayed together, we
   Will go with you along.

We have short time to stay as you;
   We have as short a spring;
As quick a growth to meet decay,
   As you or anything.
      We die,
   As your hours do, and dry
      Away
   Like to the summer's rain;
Or as the pearls of morning's dew,
   Ne'er to be found again.

How Soon Hath Time

JOHN MILTON

How soon hath Time, the subtle thief of youth,
  Stoln on his wing my three and twentieth year!
  My hasting days fly on with full career,
  But my late spring no bud or blossom shew'th.
Perhaps my semblance might deceive the truth,
  That I to manhood am arrived so near,
  And inward ripeness doth much less appear,
  That some more timely-happy spirits endu'th.
Yet be it less or more, or soon or slow,
  It shall be still in strictest measure even
  To that same lot, however mean or high,
Toward which Time leads me, and the will of Heaven;
  All is, if I have grace to use it so,
  As ever in my great Taskmaster's eye.

Life

GEORGE HERBERT

I made a posy, while the day ran by:
"Here will I smell my remnant out, and tie
    My life within this band."
But Time did beckon to the flowers, and they
By noon most cunningly did steal away,
    And withered in my hand.

My hand was next to them, and then my heart;
I took, without more thinking, in good part
    Time's gentle admonition;
Who did so sweetly death's sad taste convey,
Making my mind to smell my fatal day,
    Yet sugaring the suspicion.

Farewell dear flowers, sweetly your time ye spent,
Fit, while ye lived, for smell or ornament,
    And after death for cures.
I follow straight without complaints or grief,
Since, if my scent be good, I care not if
    It be as short as yours.

The Simple Life

Matthew 5:3-9

Blessed are the poor in spirit: for theirs is the kingdom
of heaven.

Blessed are they that mourn: for they shall be comforted.

Blessed are the meek: for they shall inherit the earth.

Blessed are they which do hunger and thirst after
righteousness: for they shall be filled.

Blessed are the merciful: for they shall obtain mercy.

Blessed are the pure in heart: for they shall see God.

Blessed are the peacemakers: for they shall be called
the children of God.

The Apology

RALPH WALDO EMERSON

Think me not unkind and rude
That I walk alone in grove and glen;
I go to the god of the wood
To fetch his word to men.

Tax not my sloth that I
Fold my arms beside the brook;
Each cloud that floated in the sky
Writes a letter in my book.

Chide me not, laborious band,
For the idle flowers I brought;
Every aster in my hand
Goes home loaded with a thought.

There was never mystery
But 't is figured in the flowers;
Was never secret history
But birds tell it in the bowers.

One harvest from thy field
Homeward brought the oxen strong;
A second crop thine acres yield,
Which I gather in a song.

Matthew 6:25-31

Therefore I say unto you, Take no thought for your life, what ye shall eat, or what ye shall drink; nor yet for your body, what ye shall put on. Is not the life more than meat, and the body than raiment? Behold the fowls of the air; for they sow not, neither do they reap, nor gather into barns; yet your heavenly Father feedeth them. Are ye not much better than they? Which of you by taking thought can add one cubit unto his stature? And why take ye thought for raiment? Consider the lilies of the field, how they grow; they toil not, neither do they spin: And yet I say unto you, That even Solomon in all his glory was not arrayed like one of these. Wherefore, if God so clothe the grass of the field, which to day is, and to morrow is cast into the oven, shall he not much more clothe you, O ye of little faith? Therefore take no thought, saying, What shall we eat? or, What shall we drink? or, Wherewithal shall we be clothed?... For your heavenly Father knoweth that ye have need of all these things.

The Passionate Shepherd

NICHOLAS BRETON

Who can live in heart so glad
As the merry country lad?
Who upon a fair green balk
May at pleasure sit and walk,
And amid the azure skies
See the morning sun arise;
While he hears in every spring
How the birds do chirp and sing;
Or before the hounds in cry
See the hare go stealing by;
Or along the shallow brook
Angling with a baited hook,
See the fishes leap and play
In a blessed sunny day;
Or to hear the partridge call
Till she have her covey all;
Or to see the subtle fox,
How the villain plies the box,
After feeding on his prey
How he closely sneaks away
Through the hedge and down the furrow,
Till he gets into his burrow;
Then the bee to gather honey,
And the little black hair'd coney

On a bank for sunny place
With her forefeet wash her face:
Are not these, with thousands moe
Than the courts of kings do know,
The true pleasing-spirits sights
That may breed true love's delights?

A Happy Life

EARL OF WESTMORLAND

That which creates a happy life
Is substance left, not gained by strife,
A fertile and a thankful mold,
A chimney always free from cold;
Never to be the client, or
But seldom times the counselor.
A mind content with what is fit,
Whose strength doth most consist in wit;
A body nothing prone to be
Sick; a prudent simplicity.
Such friends as of one's own rank are;
Homely fare, not sought from far;
The table without art's help spread;
A night in wine not buried,
Yet drowning cares; a bed that's blest
With true joy, chastity, and rest;
Such short, sweet slumber as may give
Less time to die in't, more to live:
Thine own estate whate'er commend,
And wish not for, nor fear thine end.

The Country Life, to the Honored Endymion Porter...

ROBERT HERRICK

Sweet country life, to such unknown,
Whose lives are others', not their own!
But, serving courts and cities, be
Less happy, less enjoying thee...

When now the cock, the plowman's horn,
Calls forth the lily-wrested morn,
Then to thy corn-fields thou dost go,
Which, though well soiled, yet thou dost know
That the best compost for the lands
Is the wise master's feet and hands.
There at the plow thou find'st thy team,
With a hind whistling there to them,
And cheer'st them up by singing how
The kingdom's portion is the plow...

O happy life! if that their good
The husbandmen but understood,
Who all the day themselves do please,
And younglings, with such sports as these;
And, lying down, have naught t'affright
Sweet sleep, that makes more short the night.

From The Forrest
III: To Sir Robert Wroth

BEN JONSON

How blest are thou, canst love the country, Wroth,
Whether by choice, or fate, or both;
And, though so near the city and the court,
Art ta'en with neither's vice nor sport;
That, at great times, are no ambitious guest
Of sheriff's dinner, or mayor's feast,
Nor com'st to view the better cloth of state,
The richer hangings, or crown-plate,
Nor throng'st, when masquing is, to have a sight
Of the short bravery of the night,
To view the jewels, stuffs, the pains, the wit
There wasted, some not paid for yet;
But canst at home in thy securer rest
Live, with unbought provision blessed,
Free from proud porches, or their gilded roofs,
'Mongst lowing herds and solid hoofs,
Alongst the curled woods and painted meads
Through which a serpent river leads
To some cool, courteous shade, which he calls his,
And makes sleep softer than it is!

Solitude

ALEXANDER POPE

Happy the man whose wish and care
A few paternal acres bound,
Content to breathe his native air,
In his own ground.

Whose herds with mild, whose fields with bread,
Whose flocks supply him with attire,
Whose trees in summer yield him shade,
In winter fire.

Blest, who can unconcernedly find
Hours, days, and years slide soft away,
In health of body, peace of mind,
Quiet by day.

Sound sleep by night; study and ease,
Together mixed; sweet recreation;
And innocence, which most does please
With meditation.

Thus let me live, unseen, unknown;
Thus unlamented let me die;
Steal from the world, and not a stone
Tell where I lie.

My Mind to Me a Kingdom Is

SIR EDWARD DYER

My mind to me a kingdom is;
Such perfect joy therein I find
That it excels all other bliss
That world affords or grows by kind.
Though much I want which most men have,
Yet still my mind forbids to crave.

No princely pomp, no wealthy store,
No force to win the victory,
No wily wit to salve a sore,
No shape to feed each gazing eye;
To none of these I yield as thrall.
For why my mind doth serve for all.

I see how plenty suffers oft,
How hasty climbers soon do fall;
I see that those that are aloft
Mishap doth threaten most of all;
They get with toil, they keep with fear.
Such cares my mind could never bear.

Content I live, this is my stay;
I see no more than may suffice;
I press to bear no haughty sway;

Look what I lack my mind supplies;
Lo, thus I triumph like a king,
Content with that my mind doth bring.

Some have too much, yet still do crave;
I little have, and seek no more.
They are but poor, though much they have,
And I am rich with little store.
They poor, I rich; they beg, I give;
They lack, I leave; they pine, I live.

I laugh not at another's loss;
I grudge not at another's gain;
No worldly waves my mind can toss;
My state at one doth still remain.
I fear no foe, nor fawning friend;
I loathe not life, nor dread my end.

Some weigh their pleasure by their lust,
Their wisdom by their rage of will,
Their treasure is their only trust;
And cloaked craft their store of skill.
But all the pleasure that I find
Is to maintain a quiet mind.

My wealth is health and perfect ease;
My conscience clear my chief defense;
I neither seek by bribes to please,

Nor by deceit to breed offense.
Thus do I live; thus will I die.
Would all did so as well as I!

From The Lotus Eaters
From Choric Song

ALFRED, LORD TENNYSON

I

There is a sweet music here that softer falls
Than petals from blown roses on the grass,
Or night-dews on still waters between walls
Of shadowy granite, in a gleaming pass;
Music that gentlier on the spirit lies,
Than tired eyelids upon tired eyes;
Music that brings sweet sleep down from
  the blissful skies.
Here are cool mosses deep,
and thro' the moss the ivies creep,
And in the stream the long-leaved flowers weep,
And from the craggy ledge the poppy hangs in sleep.

II

Why are we weigh'd upon with heaviness,
And utterly consumed with sharp distress,
While all things else have rest from weariness?
All things have rest: why should we toil alone,
We only toil, who are the first of things,
And make perpetual moan,
Still from one sorrow to another thrown;
Nor ever fold our wings,

And cease from wanderings,
Nor steep our brows in slumber's holy balm;
Nor harken what the inner spirit sings,
"There is no joy but calm!"—
Why should we only toil, the roof and crown of things?

Tears, Idle Tears
Songs from The Princess

ALFRED, LORD TENNYSON

Tears, idle tears, I know not what they mean,
Tears from the depth of some divine despair
Rise in the heart, and gather to the eyes,
In looking on the happy autumn-fields,
And thinking of the days that are no more.

Fresh as the first beam glittering on a sail,
That brings our friends up from the underworld,
Sad as the last which reddens over one
That sinks with all we love below the verge;
So sad, so fresh, the days that are no more.

Ah, sad and strange as in dark summer dawns
The earliest pipe of half-awakened birds
To dying ears, when unto dying eyes
The casement slowly grows a glimmering square;
So sad, so strange, the days that are no more.

Dear as remembered kisses after death,
And sweet as those by hopeless fancy feigned
On lips that are for others; deep as love,
Deep as first love, and wild with all regret;
O Death in Life, the days that are no more!

My Friend, the Things That Do Attain

HENRY HOWARD, EARL OF SURREY

My friend, the things that do attain
The happy life be these, I find:
The riches left, not got with pain;
The fruitful ground; the quiet mind;

The equal friend; no grudge, no strife;
No charge of rule, nor governance;
Without disease, the healthy life;
The household of continuance;

The mean diet, no dainty fare;
Wisdom joined with simpleness;
The night dischargéd of all care,
Where wine the wit may not oppress;

The faithful wife, without debate;
Such sleeps as may beguile the night;
Content thyself with thine estate,
Neither wish death, nor fear his might.

Song from The Indian Emperor

JOHN DRYDEN

Ah, fading joy, how quickly art thou past!
    Yet we thy ruin haste.
As if the cares of human life were few,
    We seek out new:
And follow fate, which would too fast pursue.

See how on every bough the birds express
    In their sweet notes their happiness.
    They all enjoy and nothing spare;
But on their mother nature lay their care;
Why then should man, the lord of all below,
    Such troubles choose to know
As none of all his subjects undergo?

Hark, hark, the waters fall, fall, fall,
    And with a murmuring sound
    Dash, dash upon the ground,
      To gentle slumber's call.

1263

EMILY DICKINSON

There is no Frigate like a Book
To take us Lands away
Nor any Coursers like a Page
Of prancing Poetry—
This Traverse may the poorest take
Without oppress of Toll—
How frugal is the Chariot
That bears the Human soul.

God's Gift
of Children

Childhood

DAVID BATES

Childhood, sweet and sunny childhood,
With its careless, thoughtless air,
Like the verdant, tangled wildwood,
Wants the training hand of care.

See it springing all around us
Glad to know, and quick to learn;
Asking questions that confound us;
Teaching lessons in its turn.

Who loves not its joyous revel,
Leaping lightly on the lawn,
Up the knoll, along the level,
Free and graceful as a fawn?

Let it revel; it is nature
Giving to the little dears
Strength of limb, and healthful features,
For the toil of coming years.

He who checks a child with terror,
Stops its play, and stills its song,
Not alone commits an error,
But a great and moral wrong.

Give it play, and never fear it
Active life is no defect;
Never, never break its spirit
Curb it only to direct.

Would you dam the flowing river,
Thinking it would cease to flow?
Onward it must go forever
Better teach it where to go.

Childhood is a fountain welling,
Trace its channel in the sand,
And its currents, spreading, swelling,
Will revive the withered land.

Childhood is the vernal season;
Trim and train the tender shoot;
Love is to the coming reason,
As the blossom to the fruit.

Tender twigs are bent and folded
Art to nature beauty lends;
Childhood easily is moulded;
Manhood breaks, but seldom bends.

A Boat beneath a Sunny Sky

LEWIS CARROLL

A boat beneath a sunny sky,
Lingering onward dreamily
In an evening of July

Children three that nestle near,
Eager eye and willing ear,
Pleased a simple tale to hear

Long has paled that sunny sky:
Echoes fade and memories die:
Autumn frosts have slain July.

Still she haunts me, phantomwise,
Alice moving under skies
Never seen by waking eyes.

Children yet, the tale to hear,
Eager eye and willing ear,
Lovingly shall nestle near.

In a Wonderland they lie,
Dreaming as the days go by,
Dreaming as the summers die:

Ever drifting down the stream
Lingering in the golden dream
Life, what is it but a dream?

From Songs of Innocence
Introduction

WILLIAM BLAKE

Piping down the valleys wild
Piping songs of pleasant glee
On a cloud I saw a child,
And he laughing said to me,

"Pipe a song about a Lamb";
So I piped with merry cheer.
"Piper pipe that song again"—
So I piped, he wept to hear.

"Drop thy pipe thy happy pipe"
Sing thy songs of happy cheer;
So I sung the same again
While he wept with joy to hear.

"Piper sit thee down and write
In a book that all may read"—
So he vanish'd from my sight.
And I pluck'd a hollow reed,

And I made a rural pen,
And I stain'd the water clear,

And I wrote my happy songs
Every child may joy to hear.

In Reference to Her Children

ANNE BRADSTREET

I had eight birds hatcht in one nest,
Four Cocks were there, and Hens the rest.
I nurst them up with pain and care,
No cost nor labour did I spare
Till at the last they felt their wing,
Mounted the Trees and learned to sing.

A Cradle Song

WILLIAM BLAKE

Sweet dreams form a shade,
O'er my lovely infants head.
Sweet dreams of pleasant streams,
By happy silent moony beams.

Sweet sleep with soft down,
Weave thy brows in infant crown.
Sweet sleep Angel mild,
Hover o'er my happy child.

Sweet smiles in the night,
Hover over my delight.
Sweet smiles Mothers smiles
All the livelong night beguiles.

Sweet moans, dovelike sighs,
Chase not slumber from thy eyes.
Sweet moans, sweeter smiles,
All the dovelike moans beguiles.

Sleep sleep happy child.
All creation slept and smil'd.
Sleep sleep, happy sleep,
While o'er thee thy mother weep.

Sweet babe in thy face,
Holy image I can trace.
Sweet babe once like thee,
Thy maker lay and wept for me,

Wept for me for thee for all,
When he was an infant small.
Thou his image ever see,
Heavenly face that smiles on thee.

Smiles on thee on me on all,
Who became an infant small,
Infant smiles are his own smiles,
Heaven & earth to peace beguiles.

To the Infant Martyrs

RICHARD CRASHAW

Go, smiling souls, your new-built cages break,
In heaven you'll learn to sing, ere here to speak,
Nor let the milky fonts that bathe your thirst
          Be your delay;
The place that calls you hence is, at the worst,
          Milk all the way.

Friendship

Fear Not, Dear Friend

ROBERT LOUIS STEVENSON

Fear not, dear friend, but freely live your days
Though lesser lives should suffer. Such am I,
A lesser life, that what is his of sky
Gladly would give for you, and what of praise.
Step, without trouble, down the sunlit ways.
We that have touched your raiment, are made whole
From all the selfish cankers of man's soul,
And we would see you happy, dear, or die.
Therefore be brave, and therefore, dear, be free;
Try all things resolutely, till the best,
Out of all lesser betters, you shall find;
And we, who have learned greatness from you, we,
Your lovers, with a still, contented mind,
See you well anchored in some port of rest.

He Wishes for the Cloths of Heaven

WILLIAM BUTLER YEATS

Had I the heavens' embroidered cloths,
Enwrought with golden and silver light,
The blue and the dim and the dark cloths
Of night and light and the half-light,
I would spread the cloths under your feet:
But I, being poor, have only my dreams;
I have spread my dreams under your feet;
Tread softly because you tread on my dreams.

Sonnet 30

WILLIAM SHAKESPEARE

When to the sessions of sweet silent thought
I summon up remembrance of things past,
I sigh the lack of many a thing I sought,
And with old woes new walk my dear time's waste:
Then can I drown an eye, unused to flow,
For precious friends hid in death's dateless night,
And weep afresh love's long since canceled woe,
And moan the expense of many a vanished sight:
Then can I grieve at grievances foregone,
And heavily from woe to woe tell o'er
The sad account of fore-bemoanéd moan,
Which I new pay as if not paid before.
But if the while I think on thee, dear friend,
All losses are restored and sorrows end.

Choices

The Tyger

WILLIAM BLAKE

Tyger! Tyger! burning bright
In the forests of the night,
What immortal hand or eye
Could frame thy fearful symmetry?

In what distant deeps or skies
Burnt the fire of thine eyes?
On what wings dare he aspire?
What the hand, dare seize the fire?

And what shoulder, & what art,
Could twist the sinews of thy heart?
And when thy heart began to beat,
What dread hand? & what dread feet?

What the hammer? what the chain?
In what furnace was thy brain?
What the anvil? what dread grasp
Dare its deadly terrors clasp?

When the starts threw down their spears,
And water'd heaven with their tears,
Did he smile his work to see?
Did he who made the Lamb make thee?

Tyger! Tyger! buring bright
In the forests of the night,
What immortal hand or eye
Dare frame thy fearful symmetry?

Ask Me No More

ALFRED, LORD TENNYSON

Ask me no more: the moon may draw the sea;
The cloud may stoop from heaven and take the shape,
With fold to fold, of mountain or of cape;
But O too fond, when have I answered thee?
Ask me no more.

Ask me no more: what answer should I give?
I love not hollow cheek or faded eye:
Yet, O my friend, I will not have thee die!
Ask me no more, lest I should bid thee live;
Ask me no more.

Ask me no more: thy fate and mine are sealed;
I strove against the stream and all in vain;
Let the great river take me to the main.
No more, dear love, for at a touch I yield;
Ask me no more.

Eternity

WILLIAM BLAKE

He who binds to himself a joy
Does the wingéd life destroy
But he who kisses the joy as it flies
Lives in eternity's sun rise.

1455

EMILY DICKINSON

Opinion is a flitting thing,
But Truth, outlasts the Sun—
If then we cannot own them both—
Possess the oldest one—

The Wonder of Life

Psalm 104:1-14

Bless the Lord, O my soul. O Lord my God, thou art
very great; thou art clothed with honour and majesty.
Who coverest thyself with light as with a garment:
who stretchest out the heavens like a curtain: Who
layeth the beams of his chambers in the waters: who
maketh the clouds his chariot: who walketh upon the
wings of the wind: Who maketh his angels spirits; his
ministers a flaming fire. Who laid the foundations of
the earth that it should not be removed for ever. Thou
coveredst it with the deep as with a garment: the
waters stood above the mountains. At thy rebuke they
fled; at the voice of thy thunder they hasted away.
They go up by the mountains; they go down by the valleys unto the place which thou hast founded for them.
Thou hast set a bound that they may not pass over;
that they turn not again to cover the earth. He sendeth
the springs into the valleys, which run among the hills.
They give drink to every beast of the field: the wild
asses quench their thirst. By them shall the fowls of
the heaven have their habitation, which sing among
the branches. He watereth the hills from his chambers:
the earth is satisfied with the fruit of thy works. He
causeth the grass to grow for the cattle, and herb for
the service of man: that he may bring forth food out of
the earth.

31

WALT WHITMAN

I believe a leaf of grass is no less than the journey-
  work of the stars,
And the pismire is equally perfect, and a grain of sand,
  and the egg of the wren,
And the tree-toad is a chef-d'œuvre for the highest,
And the running blackberry would adorn the parlors
  of heaven,
And the narrowest hinge in my hand puts to scorn
  all machinery,
And the cow crunching with depress'd head surpasses
  any statue,
And a mouse is miracle enough to stagger sextillions
  of infidels . . .

Miracles

WALT WHITMAN

Why, who makes much of a miracle?
As to me I know of nothing else but miracles,
Whether I walk the streets of Manhattan,
Or dart my sight over the roofs of houses toward the
    sky,
Or wade with naked feet along the beach just in the
    edge of the water,
Or stand under trees in the woods,
Or talk by day with any one I love, or sleep in the bed
    at night with any one I love,
Or sit at table at dinner with the rest,
Or look at strangers opposite me riding in the car,
Or watch honey-bees busy around the hive of a
    summer forenoon,
Or animals feeding in the fields,
Or birds, or the wonderfulness of insects in the air,
Or the wonderfulness of the sundown, or of stars shin-
    ing so quiet and bright,
Or the exquisite delicate thin curve of the new moon in
        spring;
These with the rest, one and all, are to me miracles,
The whole referring, yet each distinct and in its place.

The Wonder of Life

To me every hour of the light and dark is a miracle,
Every cubic inch of space is a miracle,
Every square yard of the surface of the earth is spread
    with the same,
Every foot of the interior swarms with the same.

To me the sea is a continual miracle,
The fishes that swim—the rocks—the motion of the
    waves—the ships with men in them,
What stranger miracles are there?

From I Sing the Body Electric
4

WALT WHITMAN

I have perceiv'd that to be with those I like is enough,
To stop in company with the rest at evening is enough,
To be surrounded by beautiful, curious, breathing,
    laughing flesh is enough,
To pass among them or touch any one, or rest my arm
    ever so lightly round his or her neck for a moment,
    what is this then?
I do not ask any more delight, I swim in it as in a sea.

There is something in staying close to men and women
    and looking on them, and in the contact and odor
    of them, that pleases the soul well,
All things please the soul, but these please the soul
    well.

God's Care

God's Lighthouses

HELEN HUNT JACKSON

When night falls on the earth, the sea
  From east to west lies twinkling bright
  With shining beams from beacons high
  Which flash afar a friendly light.
The sailor's eyes, like eyes in prayer,
  Turn unto them for guiding ray:
  If storms obscure their radiance,
  The great ships helpless grope their way.
When night falls on the earth, the sky
  Looks like a wide, a boundless main.
  Who knows what voyagers sail there?
  Who names the ports they seek and gain?
Are not the stars like beacons set
  To guide the argosies that go
  From universe to universe,
  Our little world above, below?—
On their great errands solemn bent,
  In their vast journeys unaware
  Of our small planet's name or place
  Revolving in the lower air.
O thought too vast! O thought too glad!
  An awe most rapturous it stirs.
  From world to world God's beacons shine:
  God means to save his mariners!

The Presence

JONES VERY

I sit within my room and joy to find
That Thou who always loves art with me here,
That I am never left by Thee behind,
But by Thyself Thou keep'st me ever near;
The fire turns brighter when with Thee I look,
And seems a kinder servant sent to me;
With gladder heart I read Thy holy book,
Because Thou art the eyes by which I see;
This aged chair, that table, watch, and door
Around in ready service ever wait;
Nor can I ask of Thee a menial more
To fill the measure of my large estate,
For Thou Thyself, with all a Father's care,
Where'er I turns, art ever with me there.

Behold the Child

ALEXANDER POPE

Behold the child, by Nature's kindly law,
Pleased with a rattle, tickled with a straw:
Some livelier play-thing gives his youth delight,
A little louder, but as empty quite:
Scarfs, garters, gold, amuse his riper stage,
And beads and prayer-books are the toys of age:
Pleased with this bauble still, as that before;
'Till tired he sleeps, and Life's poor play is o'er.
Meanwhile Opinion gilds with varying rays
Those painted clouds that beautify our days;
Each want of happiness by hope supplied,
And each vacuity of sense by Pride:
These build as fast as knowledge can destroy;
In Folly's cup still laughs the bubble, joy;
One prospect lost, another still we gain;
And not a vanity is given in vain;
Even mean Self-love becomes, by force divine,
The scale to measure others' wants by thine.
See! and confess, one comfort still must rise,
'Tis this, Though Man's a fool, yet GOD IS WISE.

To a Waterfowl

WILLIAM CULLEN BRYANT

Whither, midst falling dew,
While glow the heavens with the last steps of day,
Far, through their rosy depths, dost thou pursue
Thy solitary way?

Vainly the fowler's eye
Might mark thy distant flight to do thee wrong,
As, darkly painted on the crimson sky,
Thy figure floats along.

Seek'st thou the plashy brink
Of weedy lake, or marge of river wide,
Or where the rocking billows rise and sink
On the chafed ocean-side?

There is a Power whose care
Teaches thy way along that pathless coast—
The desert and illimitable air—
Lone wandering, but not lost.

All day thy wings have fanned,
At that far height, the cold, thin atmosphere,
Yet stoop not, weary, to the welcome land,
Though the dark night is near.

And soon that toil shall end;
Soon shalt thou find a summer home, and rest,
And scream among thy fellows; reeds shall bend,
Soon, o'er thy sheltered nest.

Thou'rt gone, the abyss of heaven
Hath swallowed up thy form; yet, on my heart
Deeply has sunk the lesson thou hast given,
And shall not soon depart.

He who, from zone to zone,
Guides through the boundless sky thy certain flight,
In the long way that I must tread alone,
Will lead my steps aright.

Discipline

GEORGE HERBERT

Throw away thy rod,
Throw away thy wrath:
O my God,
Take the gentle path.

For my heart's desire
Unto thine is bent:
I aspire
Not a word or look
I affect to own,
But by book,
And thy book alone.

Though I fail, I weep:
Though I halt in pace,
Yet I creep
To the throne of grace.

Then let wrath remove;
Love will do the deed:
For with love
Stony hearts will bleed.

Love is swift of foot;
Love's a man of war,
And can shoot,
And can hit from far.

Who can 'scape his bow?
That which wrought on thee,
Brought thee low,
Needs must work on me.

Throw away thy rod;
Though man frailties hath,
Thou art God:
Throw away thy wrath.

The Lamb

WILLIAM BLAKE

Little Lamb, who made thee?
Dost thou know who made thee?
Gave thee life & bid thee feed,
By the stream & o'er the mead;
Gave thee clothing of delight,
Softest clothing wooly bright:
Gave thee such a tender voice,
Making all the vales rejoice!
Little Lamb who made thee?
Dost thou know who made thee?

Little Lamb I'll tell thee,
Little Lamb I'll tell thee!
He is callèd by thy name,
For he calls himself a Lamb:
He is meek & he is mild,
He became a little child:
I a child & thou a lamb,
We are callèd by his name.
Little Lamb God bless thee.
Little Lamb God bless thee.

Trusting God

First Day Thoughts

JOHN GREENLEAF WHITTIER

In calm and cool and silence, once again
I find my old accustomed place among
My brethren, where, perchance, no human tongue
Shall utter words; where never hymn is sung,
Nor deep-toned organ blown, nor censer swung,
Nor dim light falling through the pictured pane!
There, syllabled by silence, let me hear
The still small voice which reached the prophet's ear;
Read in my heart a still diviner law
Than Israel's leader on his tables saw!
There let me strive with each besetting sin,
Recall my wandering fancies, and restrain
The sore disquiet of a restless brain;
And, as the path of duty is made plain,
May grace be given that I may walk therein,
Not like the hireling, for this selfish gain,
With backward glances and reluctant tread,
Making a merit of his coward dread,
But, cheerful, in the light around me thrown,
Walking as one to pleasant service led;
Doing God's will as if it were my own,
Yet trusting not in mine, but in His strength alone!

The Pulley

GEORGE HERBERT

When God at first made man,
Having a glass of blessings standing by,
"Let us," said he, "pour on him all we can:
Let the world's riches, which dispersed lie,
Contract into a span."

So strength first made a way;
Then beauty flowed, then wisdom, honor, pleasure.
When almost all was out, God made a stay,
Perceiving that, alone of all his treasure,
Rest in the bottom lay.

"For if I should," said he,
"Bestow this jewel also on my creature,
He would adore my gifts instead of me,
And rest in Nature, not the God of Nature;
So both should losers be.

"Yet let him keep the rest,
But keep them with repining restlessness:
Let him be rich and weary, that at least,
If goodness lead him not, yet weariness
May toss him to my breast."

Denial

GEORGE HERBERT

When my devotions could not pierce
      Thy silent ears,
Then was my heart broken, as was my verse;
My breast was full of fears
      And disorder.

My bent thoughts, like a brittle bow,
      Did fly asunder:
Each took his way; some would to pleasures go,
  Some to the wars and thunder
      Of alarms.

"As good go anywhere," they say,
      "As to benumb
Both knees and heart, in crying night and day,
  Come, come, my God, O come!
      But no hearing."

O that thou shouldst give dust a tongue
      To cry to thee,
And then not hear it crying! All day long
  My heart was in my knee,
      But no hearing.

Therefore my soul lay out of sight,
        Untuned, unstrung:
My feeble spirit, unable to look right,
  Like a nipped blossom, hung
        Discontented.

  O cheer and tune my heartless breast,
        Defer no time;
That so thy favors granting my request,
  They and my mind may chime,
        And mend my rhyme.

Psalm 121:1–8

I will lift up mine eyes unto the hills, from whence
cometh my help. My help cometh from the Lord,
which made heaven and earth. He will not suffer thy
foot to be moved: he that keepeth thee will not slumber. Behold, he that keepeth Israel shall neither slumber nor sleep. The Lord is thy keeper: the Lord is thy
shade upon thy right hand. The sun shall not smite
thee by day, nor the moon by night. The Lord shall preserve thee from all evil: he shall preserve thy soul. The
Lord shall preserve thy going out and thy coming in
from this time forth, and even for evermore.

Isaiah 55:8–12

For my thoughts are not your thoughts, neither are your ways my ways, saith the Lord. For as the heavens are higher than the earth, so are my ways higher than your ways, and my thoughts than your thoughts. For as the rain cometh down, and the snow from heaven, and returneth not thither, but watereth the earth, and maketh it bring forth and bud, that it may give seed to the sower, and bread to the eater: So shall my word be that goeth forth out of my mouth: it shall not return unto me void, but it shall accomplish that which I please, and it shall prosper in the thing whereto I sent it. For ye shall go out with joy, and be led forth with peace: the mountains and the hills shall break forth before you into singing, and all the trees of the field shall clap their hands.

Romans 8:35-39

Who shall separate us from the love of Christ? shall tribulation, or distress, or persecution, or famine, or nakedness, or peril, or sword? As it is written, For thy sake we are killed all the day long; we are accounted as sheep for the slaughter. Nay, in all these things we are more than conquerors through him that loved us. For I am persuaded, that neither death, nor life, nor angels, nor principalities, nor powers, nor things present, nor things to come, Nor height, nor depth, nor any other creature, shall be able to separate us from the love of God, which is in Christ Jesus our Lord.

God Uses Us

When I Consider How My Light Is Spent

JOHN MILTON

When I consider how my light is spent,
Ere half my days, in this dark world and wide,
And that one talent which is death to hide,
Lodged with me useless, though my soul more bent
To serve therewith my Maker, and present
My true account, lest he returning chide;
"Doth God exact day-labor, light denied?"
I fondly ask; but Patience to prevent
That murmur, soon replies, "God doth not need
Either man's work or his own gifts; who best
Bear his mild yoke, they serve him best. His state
Is kingly. Thousands at his bidding speed
And post o'er land and ocean without rest:
They also serve who only stand and wait."

The Windows

GEORGE HERBERT

Lord, how can man preach thy eternal word?
He is a brittle, crazy glass,
Yet in thy temple thou dost him afford
This glorious and transcendent place,
To be a window through thy grace.

But when thou dost anneal in glass thy story,
Making thy life to shine within
The holy preachers, then the light and glory
More revered grows, and more doth win,
Which else shows wat'rish, bleak, and thin.

Doctrine and life, colors and light, in one
When they combine and mingle, bring
A strong regard and awe; but speech alone
Doth vanish like a flaring thing,
And in the ear, not conscience, ring.

Love for God

Love I

GEORGE HERBERT

Immortal Love, author of this great frame,
Sprung from that beauty which can never fade,
How hath man parcel'd out Thy glorious name,
And thrown it on that dust which Thou hast made,
While mortal love doth all the title gain!
Which siding with Invention, they together
Bear all the sway, possessing heart and brain,
(Thy workmanship) and give Thee share in neither.
Wit fancies beauty, beauty raiseth wit;
The world is theirs, they two play out the game,
Thou standing by: though Thy glorious name
Wrought our deliverance from th' infernal pit,
Who sings Thy praise? Only a scarf or glove
Doth warm our hands, and make them write of love.

Holy Sonnets

JOHN DONNE

Batter my heart, three-personed God; for you
As yet knock, breathe, shine, and seek to mend;
That I may rise and stand, o'erthrow me, and bend
Your force to break, blow, burn, and make me new.
I, like an usurped town, to another due,
Labor to admit you, but O, to no end;
Reason, your viceroy in me, me should defend,
But is captived, and proves weak or untrue.
Yet dearly I love you, and would be loved fain,
But am betrothed unto your enemy.
Divorce me, untie or break that knot again;
Take me to you, imprison me, for I,
Except you enthrall me, never shall be free.
Nor ever chaste, except you ravish me.

God Forgives Us

A Hymn to God the Father

JOHN DONNE

Wilt thou forgive that sin where I begun,
Which is my sin, though it were done before?
Wilt thou forgive that sin through which I run,
And do run still, though still I do deplore?
When thou hast done, thou hast not done,
For I have more.
Wilt thou forgive that sin by which I have won
Others to sin? and made my sin their door?
Wilt thou forgive that sin which I did shun
A year or two, but wallowed in a score?
When thou hast done, thou hast not done,
For I have more.

I have a sin of fear, that when I have spun
My last thread, I shall perish on the shore;
Swear by thy self, that at my death thy Son
Shall shine as he shines now and hertofore;
And, having done that, thou hast done,
I fear no more.

Love III

GEORGE HERBERT

Love bade me welcome: yet my soul drew back,
Guilty of dust and sin.
But quick-eyed Love, observing me grow slack
From my first entrance in,
Drew nearer to me, sweetly questioning
If I lacked anything.

"A guest," I answered, "worthy to be here":
Love said, "You shall be he."
"I, the unkind, ungrateful? Ah, my dear,
I cannot look on thee."
Love took my hand, and smiling did reply,
"Who made the eyes but I?"

"Truth, Lord; but I have marred them; let my shame
Go where it doth deserve."
"And know you not," says Love, "who bore the
   blame?"
"My dear, then I will serve."
"You must sit down," says Love, "and taste my meat."
So I did sit and eat.

Psalm 103:1-13

Bless the Lord, O my soul: and all that is within me, bless his holy name. Bless the Lord, O my soul, and forget not all his benefits: Who forgiveth all thine iniquities; who healeth all thy diseases; Who redeemeth thy life from destruction; who crowneth thee with lovingkindness and tender mercies; Who satisfieth thy mouth with good things; so that thy youth is renewed like the eagle's. The Lord executeth righteousness and judgment for all that are oppressed. He made known his ways unto Moses, his acts unto the children of Israel. The Lord is merciful and gracious, slow to anger, and plenteous in mercy. He will not always chide: neither will he keep his anger for ever. He hath not dealt with us after our sins; nor rewarded us according to our iniquities. For as the heaven is high above the earth, so great is his mercy toward them that fear him. As far as the east is from the west, so far hath he removed our transgressions from us. Like as a father pitieth his children, so the Lord pitieth them that fear him.

A Hymn to God the Father

BEN JONSON

Hear me, O God!
A broken heart,
Is my best part;
Use still thy rod,
That I may prove
Therein thy love.

If thou hadst not
Been stern to me,
But left me free,
I had forgot
Myself and thee.

For sin's so sweet,
As minds ill bent
Rarely repent,
Until they meet
Their punishment.

Who more can crave
Than thou hast done,
That gav'st a Son,
To free a slave?
First made of naught,
With all since bought.

Sin, Death, and Hell,
His glorious Name
Quite overcame,
Yet I rebel,
And slight the same.

But I'll come in
Before my loss
Me farther toss,
As sure to win
Under his Cross.

Psalm 51:1-10

Have mercy upon me, O God, according to thy lovingkindness: according unto the multitude of thy tender mercies blot out my transgressions. Wash me throughly from mine iniquity, and cleanse me from my sin. For I acknowledge my transgressions: and my sin is ever before me. Against thee, thee only, have I sinned, and done this evil in thy sight: that thou mightest be justified when thou speakest, and be clear when thou judgest. Behold, I was shapen in iniquity; and in sin did my mother conceive me. Behold, thou desirest truth in the inward parts: and in the hidden part thou shalt make me to know wisdom. Purge me with hyssop, and I shall be clean: wash me, and I shall be whiter than snow. Make me to hear joy and gladness; that the bones which thou hast broken may rejoice. Hide thy face from my sins, and blot out all mine iniquities. Create in me a clean heart, O God; and renew a right spirit within me.

Redemption

GEORGE HERBERT

Having been tenant long to a rich lord,
   Not thriving, I resolved to be bold,
   And make a suit unto him, to afford
A new small-rented lease, and cancel the old.

In heaven at his manor I him sought;
   They told me there that he was lately gone
   About some land, which he had dearly bought
Long since on earth, to take possessiön.

I straight returned, and knowing his great birth,
   Sought him accordingly in great resorts;
   In cities, theaters, gardens, parks, and courts;
At length I heard a ragged noise and mirth
   Of thieves and murderers; there I him espied,
   Who straight, Your suit is granted, said, and died.

God Is
in Control

The Vanity of Human Wishes

Samuel Johnson

Where then shall Hope and Fear their objects find?
Must dull Suspense corrupt the stagnant mind?
Must helpless man, in ignorance sedate,
Roll darkling down, the torrent of his fate?
Must no dislike alarm, no wishes rise,
No cries invoke the mercies of the skies?
Inquirer, cease; petitions yet remain,
Which Heaven may hear, nor deem religion vain.
Still raise for good the supplicating voice,
But leave to Heaven the measure and the choice.
Safe in His power, whose eyes discern afar
The secret ambush of a specious prayer.
Implore His aid, in His decisions rest,
Secure, whate'er He gives, He gives the best.
Yet when the sense of sacred presence fires,
And strong devotion to the skies aspires,
Pour forth thy fervors for a healthful mind,
Obedient passions, and a will resigned;
For love, which scarce collective man can fill;
For patience sovereign o'er transmuted ill;
For faith, that panting for a happier seat,
Counts death kind Nature's signal of retreat:
These goods for man the laws of Heaven ordain,
These goods He grants, who grants the power to gain;

With these celestial Wisdom calms the mind,
And makes the happiness she does not find.

The Hand and Foot

JONES VERY

The hand and foot that stir not, they shall find
Sooner than all the rightful place to go:
Now in their motion free as roving wind,
Though first no snail so limited and slow;
I mark them full of labor all the day,
Each active motion made in perfect rest;
They cannot from their path mistaken stray,
Though 'tis not theirs, yet in it they are blest;
The bird has not their hidden track found out,
The cunning fox though full of art he be;
It is the way unseen, the certain route,
Where ever bound, yet thou art ever free;
The path of Him, whose perfect law of love
Bids spheres and atoms in just order move.

The Sound of the Sea

HENRY WADSWORTH LONGFELLOW

The sea awoke at midnight from its sleep,
  And round the pebbly beaches far and wide
  I heard the first wave of the rising tide
  Rush onward with uninterrupted sweep;
A voice out of the silence of the deep,
  A sound mysteriously multiplied
  As of a cataract from the mountain's side,
  Or roar of winds upon a wooded steep.
So comes to us at times, from the unknown
  And inaccessible solitudes of being,
  The rushing of the sea-tides of the soul;
And inspirations, that we deem our own,
  Are some divine foreshadowing and foreseeing
  Of things beyond our reason or control.
"Sit in reverie and watch the changing color of the
  waves that break
    upon the idle seashore of the mind."

From Olney Hymns
Light Shining out of Darkness

WILLIAM COWPER

God moves in a mysterious way,
His wonders to perform;
He plants his footsteps in the sea,
And rides upon the storm.

Deep in unfathomable mines
Of never failing skill,
He treasures up his bright designs,
And works his sovereign will.

Ye fearful saints, fresh courage take,
The clouds ye so much dread
Are big with mercy, and shall break
In blessings on your head.

Judge not the Lord by feeble sense,
But trust him for his grace;
Behind a frowning providence,
He hides a smiling face.

His purposes will ripen fast,
Unfolding every hour;

The bud may have a bitter taste,
But sweet will be the flower.

Blind unbelief is sure to err,
And scan his work in vain;
God is his own interpreter,
And he will make it plain.

Psalm 46:1–4, 10

God is our refuge and strength, a very present help in trouble. Therefore will not we fear, though the earth be removed, and though the mountains be carried into the midst of the sea; Though the waters thereof roar and be troubled, though the mountains shake with the swelling thereof. There is a river, the streams whereof shall make glad the city of God, the holy place of the tabernacles of the most High. Be still, and know that I am God: I will be exalted among the heathen, I will be exalted in the earth.

1672

EMILY DICKINSON

Lightly stepped a yellow star
To its lofty place—
Loosed the Moon her silver hat
From her lustral Face—
All of Evening softly lit
As an Astral Hall—
Father, I observed to Heaven,
You are punctual.

Psalm 23

The Lord is my shepherd; I shall not want. He maketh me to lie down in green pastures: he leadeth me beside the still waters. He restoreth my soul: he leadeth me in the paths of righteousness for his name's sake. Yea, though I walk through the valley of the shadow of death, I will fear no evil: for thou art with me; thy rod and thy staff they comfort me. Thou preparest a table before me in the presence of mine enemies: thou anointest my head with oil; my cup runneth over. Surely goodness and mercy shall follow me all the days of my life: and I will dwell in the house of the Lord for ever.

1287

EMILY DICKINSON

In this short Life
That only lasts an hour
How much—how little—is
Within our power

Thanksgiving

A Thanksgiving to God for His House

ROBERT HERRICK

Lord, Thou has given me a cell
Wherein to dwell;
A little house, whose humble roof
Is weather-proof;
Under the spars of which I lie
Both soft and dry;
Where Thou, my chamber for to ward,
Hast set a guard
Of harmless thoughts, to watch and keep
Me while I sleep.
Low is my porch, as is my fate,
Both void of state;
And yet the threshold of my door
Is worn by the poor
Who thither come, and freely get
Good words, or meat.
Like as my parlor, so my hall
And kitchen's small;
A little buttery, and therein
A little bin,
Which keeps my little loaf of bread
Unchipped, unflead;
Some brittle sticks of thorn or brier
Make me a fire,

Close by whose living coal I sit,
And glow like it...
Lord, 'tis Thy plenty-dropping hand
That soils my land,
And giv'st me, for my bushel sown,
Twice ten for one;
Thou mak'st my teeming hen to lay
Her egg each day;
Besides my healthful ewes to bear
Me twins each year;
The while the conduits of my kine
Run cream, for wine.
All these, and better, Thou dost send
Me, to this end,
That I should render, for my part,
A thankful heart;
Which, fired with incense, I resign
As wholly Thine;
But the acceptance, that must be,
My Christ, by Thee.

From Prometheus Unbound
Act II: Scene V

PERCY BYSSHE SHELLEY

Life of Life! thy lips enkindle
With their love the breath between them;
And thy smiles before they dwindle
Make the cold air fire; then screen them
In those looks, where whoso gazes
Faints, entangled in their mazes.

Child of Light! thy limbs are burning
Through the vest which seems to hide them;
As the radiant lines of morning
Through the clouds ere they divide them;
And this atmosphere divinest
Shrouds thee wheresoe'er thou shinest.

Fair are others; none beholds thee,
But thy voice sounds low and tender
Like the fairest, for it folds thee
From the sight, that liquid splendor,
And all feel, yet see thee never,
As I feel now, lost forever!

Lamp of Earth! where'er thou movest
Its dim shapes are clad with brightness,

And the souls of whom thou lovest
Walk upon the winds with lightness,
Till they fail, as I am failing,
Dizzy, lost, yet unbewailing!

Pied Beauty

GERARD MANLEY HOPKINS

Glory be to God for dappled things—
For skies of couple-colour as a brinded cow;
For rose-moles all in stipple upon trout that swim;
Fresh-firecoal chestnut-falls; finches' wings;
Landscape plotted and pieced—fold, fallow, and
   plough,
And all trades, their gear and tackle and trim.
All things counter, original, spare, strange;
Whatever is fickle, freckled (who knows how?)
With swift, slow; sweet, sour; adazzle, dim;
He fathers-forth whose beauty is past change:
Praise him.

Psalm 150

Praise ye the Lord. Praise God in his sanctuary: praise him in the firmament of his power. Praise him for his mighty acts: praise him according to his excellent greatness. Praise him with the sound of the trumpet: praise him with the psaltery and harp. Praise him with the timbrel and dance: praise him with stringed instruments and organs. Praise him upon the loud cymbals: praise him upon the high sounding cymbals. Let every thing that hath breath praise the Lord. Praise ye the Lord.

Longing
for Heaven

They Desire a Better Country

CHRISTINA ROSSETTI

1

I would not if I could undo my past,
Tho' for its sake my future is a blank;
My past for which I have myself to thank,
For all its faults and follies first and last.
I would not cast anew the lot once cast,
Or launch a second ship for one that sank,
Or drug with sweets the bitterness I drank,
Or break by feasting my perpetual fast.
I would not if I could: for much more dear
Is one remembrance than a hundred joys,
More than a thousand hopes in jubilee;

2

What seekest thou, far in the unknown land:
In hope I follow joy gone on before;
In hope and fear persistent more and more,
As the dry desert lengthens out its sand.
Whilst day and night I carry in my hand
The golden key to ope the golden door
Of golden home; yet mine eye weepeth sore,
For long the journey is that makes no stand.
And who is this that veiled doth walk with thee?
Lo, this is Love that walketh at my right;

One exile holds us both, and we are bound
To selfsame home-joys in the land of light.
Weeping thou walkest with him; weepeth he?—
Some sobbing weep, some weep and make no sound.

3
A dimness of a glory glimmers here
Thro' veils and distance from the space remote,
A faintest far vibration of a note
Reaches to us and seems to bring us near;
Causing our face to glow with braver cheer,
Making the serried mist to stand afloat,
Subduing languor with an antidote,
And strengthening love almost to cast out fear:
Till for one moment golden city walls
Rise looming on us, golden walls of home,
Light of our eyes until the darkness falls;
Then thro' the outer darkness burdensome
I hear again the tender voice that calls,
"Follow me hither, follow, rise, and come."

A Prospect of Heaven Makes Death Easy

Isaac Watts

There is a land of pure delight
Where saints immortal reign;
Infinite day excludes the night,
And pleasures banish pain.

There everlasting spring abides,
And never-withering flowers;
Death like a narrow sea divides
This heavenly land from ours.

Sweet fields beyond the swelling flood
Stand dressed in living green:
So to the Jews old Canaan stood,
While Jordan rolled between.

But timorous mortals start and shrink
To cross this narrow sea,
And linger shivering on the brink,
And fear to launch away.

Oh could we make our doubts remove,
These gloomy doubts that rise,
And see the Canaan that we love,
With unbeclouded eyes;

Could we but climb where Moses stood
And view the landscape o'er,
Not Jordan's stream, nor death's cold flood,
Should fright us from the shore.

Revelation 21:1–4

And I saw a new heaven and a new earth: for the first heaven and the first earth were passed away; and there was no more sea. And I John saw the holy city, new Jerusalem, coming down from God out of heaven, prepared as a bride adorned for her husband. And I heard a great voice out of heaven saying, Behold, the tabernacle of God is with men, and he will dwell with them, and they shall be his people, and God himself shall be with them, and be their God. And God shall wipe away all tears from their eyes; and there shall be no more death, neither sorrow, nor crying, neither shall there be any more pain: for the former things are passed away.

Ah Sun-flower

WILLIAM BLAKE

Ah Sun-flower! weary of time,
Who countest the steps of the Sun,
Seeking after that sweet golden clime
Where the traveller's journey is done;

Where the Youth pined away with desire,
And the pale Virgin shrouded in snow,
Arise from their graves and aspire,
Where my Sun-flower wishes to go.

Up-Hill

CHRISTINA ROSSETTI

Does the road wind up-hill all the way?
  Yes, to the very end.
Will the day's journey take the whole long day?
  From morn to night, my friend.

But is there for the night a resting-place?
  A roof for when the slow dark hours begin.
May not the darkness hide it from my face?
  You cannot miss that inn.

Shall I meet other wayfarers at night?
  Those who have gone before.
Then must I knock, or call when just in sight?
  They will not keep you standing at that door.

Shall I find comfort, travel-sore and weak?
  Of labor you shall find the sum.
Will there be beds for me and all who seek?
  Yea, beds for all who come.

Indices

Index of Poems by Author

Index of Poems by Author

Index of Poems by Author

Index of Poems by Title

Index of Poems by Title

Index of Poems by Title